COMMUNICATIVE AMERICAN ENGLISH

Instructor's Manual

GRETE ROLAND

National Textbook Company
a division of *NTC Publishing Group* • Lincolnwood, Illinois USA

Cover Photos by Jeff Ellis

Published by National Textbook Company, a division of NTC Publishing Group.
© 1992 by NTC Publishing Group, 4255 West Touhy Avenue,
Lincolnwood (Chicago), Illinois 60646-1975 U.S.A.
All rights reserved. No part of this book may be reproduced, stored
in a retrieval system, or transmitted in any form or by any means,
electronic, mechanical, photocopying, recording or otherwise, without
the prior permission of NTC Publishing Group.
Manufactured in the United States of America.

1 2 3 4 5 6 7 8 9 0 VP 9 8 7 6 5 4 3 2 1

Contents

Introduction   1
    The Dialogues   2

Methodology   4
    The Dialogues: Preparation and Presentation   4
    Vocabulary Building and Use of the Glossaries   4
    The Comprehension Questions   6
    The Dialogues: Practice and Pronunciation   6
    The Role Plays   9
    The Discussion Topics   10

Sample Lesson: "Learning English"   12
    Introducing Unit 4, "Being a Student"   12
    The Dialogue   12
    The Vocabulary Exercise   13
    The Comprehension Questions   14
    The Dialogue: Choral Practice   14
    The Dialogue: Pronunciation   17
    The Role Play   18
    The Discussion Topics   19

Testing Suggestions   22

Unit Descriptions   24

Lesson Notes and Activities   26
    Unit 1: Family Relationships   26
    Unit 2: Making Friends and Getting Together   28
    Unit 3: Romantic Intentions   31
    Unit 4: Being a Student   34
    Unit 5: The World of Work   40
    Unit 6: In and Around the City   43
    Unit 7: Cultural Differences and Reactions   47
    Unit 8: Recreation, Vacation, and Sports   50
    Unit 9: The Media   52
    Unit 10: Politics   54

Appendices   56
    Appendix A: Criteria for Evaluating Oral Reports   56
    Appendix B: Model Records Keeper's Outline   58
    Appendix C: Model Cloze and Vocabulary Matching Tests   59

Introduction

Communicative American English is a conversation and vocabulary program for students of American English at the intermediate and advanced levels. It consists of the student text with its fifty dialogue lessons; this instructor's manual; and two audiocassettes that provide natural, realistic interpretations of the dialogues.

This instructor's manual provides important information about the structure and methodology of *Communicative American English,* as well as strategies for presenting the course content. It includes a detailed sample lesson with step-by-step procedures for the less experienced teacher. It also provides teaching notes and in- and out-of-class activities to accompany each lesson in the student textbook. A section on testing contains suggestions for evaluating students' acquisition of the material and development of communicative skills. An overview of each unit is also included to aid in lesson planning.

Course Length

The student text intentionally contains more material than can be covered in a one-term course of four fifty-minute class periods a week. This wealth of material allows each instructor to choose the dialogue lessons that will best serve his or her class, since topics that are interesting or humorous to one instructor or class may not be so to another. The entire text can be completed in approximately ninety hours, making it suitable for a full-year course in speaking, listening, and vocabulary acquisition.

Organization and Goals of the Course

The fifty dialogue lessons are contained in ten thematic units. Each lesson in the student text includes a dialogue, a vocabulary building exercise, comprehension questions, a role-play situation, and at least two discussion topics. Follow-up questions and additional activities are provided in this manual.

The primary goal of *Communicative American English* is to build fluency and cultural understanding by means of dialogues and related activities. The dialogues provide practice in a variety of language functions. In addition, they include figurative expressions, idioms, two- and three-word verbs, proverbs, and common sayings. Studying the vernacular or spoken American English enables students to communicate effectively in school, at work, and in the community. Students will also learn to cope with the barrage of slang and colloquial expressions that confronts them in the media (TV, radio, newspapers, and magazines).

Knowledge of the vernacular also enhances creative and informal writing. Expressive writing is the first step toward the development of a formal writing style, the gateway to thinking through writing in English. Since the vernacular is riddled with clichés and colloquialisms, however, it is inappropriate in strictly academic and formal writing. This dichotomy of language usage, common in the languages of the world, must be clarified at the start of the course, and students should be reminded of it from time to time.

THE DIALOGUES

Cultural Content

The fifty dialogues in *Communicative American English* portray social and cultural situations as well as psychological states of being. Each dialogue contains cultural markers that encourage discussion of differences among cultures. In addition, Unit 7 ("Cultural Differences and Reactions") treats subjects of special concern to people of minority cultures living in the United States. Topics covered in this unit include introductions, nicknames, gender differences in attitudes and behavior, regional differences, privacy, and food.

Language Functions

The dialogues also illustrate a variety of language functions, such as complaining, persuading, giving advice, showing respect, and arguing. The specific language functions used in each dialogue are listed in the "Lesson Notes and Activities" section of this instructor's manual.

Figurative Expressions

The figurative expressions and terms used in the dialogues are defined in the student text glossaries, one covering animal-based expressions and the other focusing on additional idiomatic words and expressions. Expressions listed in the latter glossary are also defined following the dialogues in which they appear.

Vulgar terms have been avoided throughout the text; students who inquire about them should be advised to consult either the dictionary or the original source where they heard or saw the expression. You may wish to give a mini-lesson on insults, vulgarisms, and ethnic slurs if appropriate. Discussing ethnic slurs can be valuable, for it leads to analysis of prejudice, discrimination, and racism. In such a discussion, it is wise to take a global perspective initially. Your acknowledgment of ethnic conflict in the community and your humane and fair-minded stand (undergirded by such documents as the U.S. Bill of Rights, the U.S. Civil Rights Act, the U.N. Declaration of Human Rights) can only improve the teacher-student relationship. Ignoring social realities may distance you from your students; talking about them often creates an improved affective environment.

Characters' Names

The names of the characters in the dialogues have been carefully selected to minimize gender stereotyping and to facilitate performance of the dialogues by students of either sex. Some of the names are gender-neutral; for example, *Pat* and *Chris*. The others are members of male and female quasi-phonetic pairs. Refer to the list below for help in matching the gender of the students performing a dialogue to their characters.

Female	Male
Ann	Andy
Barbara	Barry
Betty	Bob
Carol	Carl
Helen	Henry
Joan	John
Josie	Joe
Joyce	Jack
Luisa	Luís
Louise	Lou
Maria	Mario
Mattie	Mat
Stella	Steve
Susan	Sam
Tara	Tom

As an alternative, the dialogues may be personalized by allowing the students to use their own names.

Methodology

THE DIALOGUES: PREPARATION AND PRESENTATION

As you begin each lesson, prepare the students for the dialogue topic by making general statements about the theme and by asking students questions about similar experiences they've had. Specific suggestions for introducing each dialogue are provided in the "Lead-in" for each lesson in the "Lesson Notes and Activities" section of this manual. You may also wish to use the material in the "Unit Descriptions" section of this manual when introducing a new unit.

Read the dialogue to the class at least twice, using natural, conversational speech and changing your voice and/or head movement for each character. It's a good idea to make some physical indication of the change of speakers. One of my colleagues actually changes hats and scarves. Another colleague prefers to use stick paper dolls. He holds up a stick (with a paper doll pasted to it) while he is speaking for one character, then he holds up another stick for a different character, and continues in this way as he alternates between the speaking parts.

During the second reading, check for comprehension of the characters, the situation, the underlying or double meanings, and the vocabulary, including the figurative expressions and idioms. This leads naturally to the Vocabulary Building exercise, which you and the students should do next.

VOCABULARY BUILDING AND USE OF THE GLOSSARIES

The figurative expressions and idioms featured in each dialogue are defined in the glossaries at the back of the student textbook. The vocabulary building exercise is especially designed to utilize the main glossary of animal-based expressions. The glossary of idioms and other expressions serves as a convenience for student reference; the expressions included in that glossary are also defined following each dialogue in which they appear.

The main glossary contains a wealth of expressions, not all of which appear in the dialogue. Through use of this glossary, students will find the freedom to take risks, to explore, and to experiment with English in their role plays, discussions, and activities. Names of animals are listed alphabetically in the glossary, followed by figurative expressions using each animal name. For the most part, the animal is the origin of every term and expression that follows it. However, a few expressions of dubious etymological origin and/or not actually relating to the animal are included so that students may associate them with the animal as a mnemonic device. The figurative expressions for each animal are organized by parts of speech: nouns; verbs; adjective modifiers; adverb modifiers; and proverbs and sayings. If you "walk the students through" the use of the glossary at first, soon they will use it quickly and effectively on their own.

Begin the vocabulary building exercise by having the students copy each expression or term in a notebook. Another idea is to use index cards, one expression or term per card. (Index cards can be easily carried to study on buses or trains and while waiting in lines.) Below each expression, the students should copy the line from the dialogue that contains the term. They should also note its part of speech. Next, have the students turn to the glossary and find the animal mentioned in the term or expression. When all the students have the page open to the correct animal, direct them to the appropriate part of speech and have a volunteer read the correct definition. The students should copy down the definition, synonym, or synonymous phrase that fits the usage in the dialogue. Intermediate-level students may wish to add a definition in their first language. Discourage advanced students from doing this; it distracts them from thinking in English.

The students should add to their notes any other clarification or example given in class as well as the title and page number of the dialogue in which the expression appeared.

If the term later appears elsewhere, the new definition or synonym should be numbered and added to the student's notes for the expression. Immediately writing down all the possible definitions or synonyms for a term proves much too confusing and retards retention. It is more effective to learn meanings one at a time with the memory "hooks" developed by contextual comprehension, practice, and usage. With time, as the students' vocabulary builds, their notes for a particular expression will likewise expand.

The definitions, synonyms, and synonymous phrases in the glossary are presented using formal language. Point this out to the students and encourage them to distinguish between formally written and informally spoken American English. Demonstrate some differences in language, style, and structure by taking a few lines from the dialogue and rewriting them as expository prose; for example, below is an expository version of "Patty, My Sister" from Unit One.

> My sister Patty is so childish. The reason I believe this is that she wears pigtails at the age of sixteen! She also chews her fingernails. She has another disagreeable trait. She lives extravagantly. She weasels money out of our mother to squander on clothes and junk food. Mother has told her to get a part-time job; however, Patty just wormed another ten dollars out of her. If Mother does not discipline her and refuse to give her money, I will have to do something about this problem. Otherwise, my sister will never grow up and become independent.

As with most languages of the world, formal English is appropriate for academic and business writing, while informal English is appropriate for speech as well as for expressive and creative writing. Point out that the short answers and sentence fragments of spoken English have no place in formal, expository writing, which lacks the context of human speech and nonverbal communication.

THE COMPREHENSION QUESTIONS

When the students have listened to the dialogue twice and completed the vocabulary building exercise, ask them to answer the comprehension questions. If you have already asked a couple of the questions in general class discussion or in the process of doing the vocabulary building exercise, repeat them now or have the students ask each other the questions. Using the comprehension questions enhances understanding of the situation and the characters. Although most of the questions ask for information about the dialogue, some are intended to elicit student opinions. The questions may lead to additional class discussion and sharing of similar experiences. Younger students often respond well to personalizing; but take caution with older, adult students. Some do not appreciate intrusive questions about their private lives.

Also, you may need to be cautious about calling on individual students by name, a practice considered insulting in some cultures. The cross-cultural knowledge and maturity of your students, along with their language level, should determine whether you call on individual students by name, set up partnerships in which students ask each other questions, or "throw out" a question to the entire class. When you ask the class a question, encourage all the students to respond, but don't insist. Without calling out names, you can still acknowledge correct answers. As the students gain confidence, give them the chance to ask the comprehension questions.

New students should be allowed to learn for a certain period of time simply by listening passively, unless they volunteer to participate actively. You should, however, consult privately with any student who has been in an English-speaking country for six months or longer or has studied English for several years and still does not participate after a couple of sessions. The materials may be too advanced; the student may have good comprehension but just need more time to adjust to the situation; or you may be asking the questions and expecting the answers too fast. A frequent complaint of ESL and EFL students is that the teacher talks too fast. Ask each question at a moderate pace the first time, and then repeat it at a normal, conversational speed before expecting an answer. Avoid rephrasing a question when you repeat it, unless you are careful to use lower-level vocabulary words, not idioms.

After completing the comprehension questions, you may wish to use the "Follow-up" questions provided for each lesson in the "Lesson Notes and Activities" section of this manual. The follow-ups stimulate further analysis and discussion of each dialogue situation.

THE DIALOGUES: PRACTICE AND PRONUNCIATION

At this point you can assume that the students have understood the dialogue. The next step is for them to learn the dialogue using either an active or a passive approach.

The active approach makes use of a technique called "choral practice." Choral practice has a two-fold purpose: to attain fluency and to achieve accuracy of pronunciation. By conducting the students as though they were learning a choral piece, you may tap their home cultural experience. In the West the tradition harkens back to Greek drama, but it is far older than that and still prevalent in the Middle East and the Far East. Consequently, it appeals to many students. They may have experienced it formally in their religion and at school, or they may have experienced it informally during play. Many students' ears are attuned to the chanting of Christian, Buddhist, Hebrew, or Moslem prayer. Many have enjoyed the choral approach in the performances of traditional drama. Rote memorization, a simpler type of choral work, is a major pedagogical approach worldwide. However, while the class works at memorizing a dialogue in this disciplined, time-worn, and familiar way, the content adds a touch of humor, encouraging the students to have a good time as they work together.

Begin your choral practice by asking the students to close their books or cover the dialogue. Divide the class into groups and follow the choral technique of "backward build-up," in which you say each line of the dialogue in phrases, starting from the end of the line, and the students repeat after you. (See the sample lesson in this manual for a detailed example of the backward build-up technique.) Various group division strategies may be used: (1) dividing the class into two groups for the choral work; (2) dividing half the class (the more confident students) into dialogue groups while the other half listens and provides feedback; and (3) dividing the class into pairs or threes to perform the dialogue in turns. Another variation is to divide the class into four groups and let each group practice a different dialogue while you move from group to group checking on pronunciation and comprehension. For review, individual students may direct the class in a choral reading of a previously learned dialogue. Whichever group division is chosen, this structured learning of the dialogues purposely contrasts with the more open-ended role plays and discussions included in each lesson.

In this active, in-class memorization of a dialogue, you should assume the role of choral conductor. Use appropriate gestures both to highlight the meaning of the lines and to cue each group. At the same time, you should judge the students' performance by being attuned to individual voices within the "chorus." Work enthusiastically with the deliberate use of intonation, stress-timed rhythm, and nonverbal cues as the students repeat the dialogue phrase by phrase and then line by line. Have all the students repeat your corrections, even if you hear only one or two students making a mistake. After the choral memorization of the dialogue, have partners perform it for the class with prompting from you as needed.

After the students have memorized and practiced the dialogue, explain or review the features of pronunciation. Professor Wayne B. Dickerson makes a strong case for teaching stress and rhythm patterns in his work, *Stress in the Speech Stream: The Rhythm of Spoken English* (University of Illinois Press, 1989). Correct use of these patterns is essential for intelligibility.

Three important stress-timed rhythm characteristics are *alternation, timing,* and *squeezing*. *Alternation* refers to contrasts between stressed and unstressed syllables and between heavily and lightly stressed syllables. *Timing* (or *stress timing*) depends on the intervals of time between heavily stressed syllables. The regular beat of the rhythm is determined by the heavy stresses. *Squeezing* involves compression of unstressed syllables to keep a regular beat. There are several methods of squeezing:

8   Methodology

1. Reduction: reducing the duration of a sound

    Vowel reduction: using /ə/ or shortened versions of other vowels for all soft function words and all unstressed syllables of polysyllabic content words (for example: poss**i**ble)

    Consonant reduction: the voiced flap found in "city," "ma**dd**er" "a lot of," and "shoul**d**'ve"

2. Linking: connecting word endings to word beginnings to avoid time gaps and rearticulations. Links follow special patterns based on vowel (v) and consonant (c) sounds:

V‿V or /w,h,y,r/	go‿on and try‿it, we‿yelled so‿hard
C‿V or /w,h,y,r/	washed‿windows, a mind‿reader, Is‿it cold?
C‿C (same sounds)	this‿song, black‿coffee, in‿November
C (stop) C (stop)	to cut‿corners, stop‿crying. the Pink‿Panther
C‿C (same or similar point of articulation)	some‿boys, in‿the, long‿gone

3. Blending: two sounds change to become one. (Palatal blending is a characteristic of American English but not of British English.) For example:

/t/ + you/your = /č/	Don't‿you see? Is that‿your coat?
/d/ + you/your = /ǰ/	We sold‿your house. Did you‿like it?
/s/ + you/your = /š/	in case‿you forget to erase‿your name
/z/ + your/your = /ž/	I advise‿you to close‿your eyes.

4. Trimming: dropping sounds from the speech stream

    Contractions: "I'm," "You've," "we're," "they'll," "can't," etc.

    h-elision: "he," "him," "his," "her," and the auxiliaries "has," "had," and "have" in non-initial, unstressed positions (I told h̶im Bill h̶ad seen h̶er.)

    V-elision without syllabics: "bus**i**ness," "ev**e**ry," "trav**e**ler"

    V-elision with syllabics: "gard**e**n," "bitt**e**n," "ped**a**l," "fiddl**e**"

    Consonant cluster simplification: /t/ and /d/ are dropped from final Ct and Cd clusters (even when the /t/ and /d/ are spelled with -ed), except in clusters with /nt/, /lt/, /rt/, and /rd/ and before words beginning with a vowel, or /w,h,y,r/. They regularly drop before all other consonants: for example, slep̶t soundly las̶t night.

Consult *Stress in the Speech Stream: The Rhythm of Spoken English* (Dickerson, 1989) for more information. As a rule of thumb, students should not be corrected for mispronouncing discrete phonemes unless the mispronunciation could be mistaken for a vulgarism (as with /s/ and /š/ in *sitting/shitting*) or could lead to some other gross misunderstanding.

The final step in active learning is for the students to perform the dialogues. Students at the intermediate level can be tested on their performances at designated times, when you randomly select a dialogue for them to present from those memorized in class. Your evaluation can include preparedness; naturalness of delivery; and use of correct stress, intonation, and rhythm patterns. Students should be encouraged to ad lib or extend the dialogues. After a performance, feedback from classmates is invaluable.

For the passive approach to learning a dialogue, a laboratory situation is suitable. The students listen to the dialogues on the audiocassettes. During or after listening, they should write the vocabulary building exercise and answers to the comprehension questions. In class they may take turns reading the dialogue, receiving feedback from the class and the teacher regarding the natural flow of language and proper stress-timed rhythm and intonation. If possible, arrange for the students to record themselves reading the dialogue in the language laboratory and/or performing it in class. Listening to themselves will encourage the students to develop and use their own "personal monitors," an important technique for self-correction. The advantage of learning a dialogue passively is maximum exposure to the figurative and conversational expressions in the shortest amount of time. The disadvantages lie in diminished retention of content, fluency of language, and accuracy of pronunciation.

THE ROLE PLAYS

Every lesson includes directions for one role play or sketch, usually a takeoff of the dialogue. The instructions designate the number of people needed, the specific roles to be played, and the situation. The majority of the roles are neutral; that is, they may be filled by either a male or a female. The remainder are nearly evenly divided by gender. The role play situations are open-ended, so that students may take any direction and conclude or resolve their sketches in any way they choose.

In preparing their sketches, the students can borrow lines from the lesson dialogue and refer to the glossaries for additional vocabulary. The role plays provide an opportunity for students to take risks, to collaborate, and to negotiate meaning—all necessary aspects of second language acquisition. Encourage the students to be creative, to add or omit roles to suit their purposes (but make sure every student has a part to play). You may wish to have the groups write out the dialogue for their sketches as a memory aid in case you run out of class time and some groups must perform at the following class session. You may even choose to have the groups hand in their dialogues for teacher comments before performing them for the class. Allow the groups time to practice their role plays before performing. Observe each group of students and be responsive to individual group's needs for more teacher guidance, help in visualization through writing, more freedom to create, and so forth.

Instruct the students to come to a resolution in their role plays. The situations deal with resolving conflicts, predicting outcomes, reasoning toward logical conclusions, philosophizing, and other useful communication skills. Working together and thinking in English aids students' comprehension and fluency. The students also enjoy seeing their classmates' versions of the role play and may want to make comments or ask questions about them. Therefore, provide time for feedback, spontaneous reactions, and comments after the role plays are presented.

THE DISCUSSION TOPICS

Each lesson in the student text includes two or three topics to be used as springboards for whole-class or small-group discussions. Discussion groups of three to five students are especially successful when each group chooses a group representative (the Group Rep) and a recorder (the Records Keeper) and the group members choose a topic to discuss.

The Group Rep's role is to involve every group member in the discussion. This is done by asking each person questions to elicit his or her opinions and comments. The Group Rep should paraphrase each response to check the person's intended meaning; for example, "Are you saying that _____?" or "It seems to me you believe that _____." Some group members may need to learn the importance of active participation. The Group Rep helps them by maintaining good eye contact while asking the questions as well as by paraphrasing the answers and even, if necessary, "putting words in someone's mouth" to check for intended meaning. If there is too much agreement within a group and the discussion falters, the Group Rep should play devil's advocate. Finally, the Group Rep will give an oral summary of the discussion to the class.

Meanwhile you, as a facilitator, visit each group and assume the leadership duties of the Group Rep if necessary, in order to model techniques such as playing devil's advocate. After twenty to thirty minutes of discussion, have the class form a large circle to hear the oral reports given by the Group Reps. These talks should be limited to five minutes each. (One to three minutes is usually the average.)

The responsibility of the Records Keeper is to submit a written report of the discussion in outline form. The group members' names, the discussion question, the major points and decisions made, and any recommendations for action should all be included. The Records Keeper may take a more or less passive role in the discussion but should be given time outside of class to prepare the final report; therefore, the outlines should be due at the next class session.

As many students as possible should be given the opportunity to be a Group Rep and a Records Keeper. When the students have become adept at performing these roles, the oral and written reports may serve as areas for evaluation. (See Appendices A and B for information about evaluating and for a sample written outline.)

The discussions prepare students for academic participation and for community and civic involvement. For this reason, the discussions should never be confused with conversations, which have no specific purpose other than socializing. Students in a discussion group should be asked to write out and state the discussion question, and after a discussion session the Group Rep should restate the discussion question before presenting the oral summary and declaring whether or not the group has accomplished the discussion goal—that is, answered the discussion question.

To summarize the stages in informal group discussion, the students first take part in a short *friendly exchange,* just warming up. Second, they decide on the group members' *initial responsibilities* and choose and write out the *discussion question.* Third, they *express their opinions (agreements and disagreements).* Fourth, they use *persuasion* (try to convince those who do not agree with them). Fifth, they *compromise,* and finally they *reach solutions* to problems or *make recommendations* for action.

After finishing the discussions, you may wish to conclude the lesson by using one or more of the activities presented in the "Lesson Notes and Activities" section of this manual. These varied and enjoyable activities reinforce and build on the material in each lesson and encourage students to apply that material to the world outside the classroom.

Sample Lesson: "Learning English"

This lesson is found on pages 42–43 of the student book. Throughout the sample lesson, bold type indicates what the instructor should say.

INTRODUCING UNIT 4, "BEING A STUDENT"

Paraphrase the appropriate information from the "Unit Descriptions" section of this manual: **How many years have you spent in school?** [Acknowledge voluntary student responses.] **As students in the United States, you have to devote a lot of time and energy to studying. At the same time, school is a place that brings together many different people not only for studying but also for socializing. You need to learn to manage your time well and to build good relationships with fellow students and with your teachers or professors. In this unit on "Being a Student," you will explore ways of balancing academic and social life.**

THE DIALOGUE

Ask students the Lead-in questions from the "Lesson Notes and Activities" section of this manual. **The lesson for today is called "Learning English." I am going to read the dialogue, so please listen carefully. After I read it, we will talk about the situation and the vocabulary. Then I will read it again and ask you some questions to make sure you understand. The dialogue is between Mario and Chris.** [Read the dialogue, indicating clearly the shift in the two roles; for example: change your tone of voice and/or move your head to one side for Mario and to the other for Chris. See additional suggestions in the "Methodology" section of this manual.]

MARIO:	English is driving me crazy!
CHRIS:	What's wrong?
MARIO:	I thought I knew the meaning of "foxy."
CHRIS:	Oh, yes. We talked about it yesterday in class.
MARIO:	I don't understand it anymore. I got in Dutch with my girlfriend when I said our secretary was foxy.
CHRIS:	You must be kidding! She *is* foxy.
MARIO:	Yes, but which one—clever or good-looking?
CHRIS:	Actually, both.

What does Mario mean by "English is driving me crazy"? [Wait for student responses.] That's right. He is confused. He is not very happy with learning English. Something is wrong. He got in Dutch with his girlfriend. What does "in Dutch" mean? [Wait for response.] OK, he is in trouble with her. Do you agree with Mario's statement about learning English? [Elicit responses and examples of misunderstandings your students have experienced.]

THE VOCABULARY EXERCISE

Vocabulary Building

Check the glossary for the definitions of these terms:

▶ to be kidding (v.)

▶ foxy (adj.)

Write a synonym or synonymous phrase for each term in your notebook.

Other Expressions

to drive someone crazy   *to annoy or disturb someone*

in Dutch   *in trouble*

Let's look up the animal-based expressions in the glossary, first "to be kidding." What does it mean? [Wait for students to find the answer. If no response, direct them to the correct page and have a student read the definition and/or synonym. Then tell the students to copy it in their notebooks or on a vocabulary card.]
The next animal-based expression is "foxy." Where can you find it in the glossary? Let's look it up. [Follow the above procedure until all the terms have been looked up and written down.]
Now read the "Other Expressions" and their meanings. [pause] Does anyone have a question about these expressions?

14   Sample Lesson: "Learning English"

THE COMPREHENSION QUESTIONS

Questions

1. Why is English driving Mario crazy?
2. How did Mario get in Dutch with his girlfriend?
3. How could Mario have avoided this problem?
4. Why do you think Mario's girlfriend got angry? Do you think her reaction was justified?
5. What does Chris think about the secretary?

I'm going to ask you these questions to be sure you understand the dialogue. [Ask the class the questions and allow a reasonable time for them to respond to each one together or individually.]
   Now I'm going to read the entire dialogue again. Listen carefully. After I finish, you will have a chance to ask questions. [Read the dialogue a second time and ask the students if they have any questions.]

THE DIALOGUE: CHORAL PRACTICE

Now we'll practice the dialogue together. Let's make two groups, one group for each character. Keep your books closed. [Rearrange seats if necessary. Have the groups face each other.]
Listen and repeat after me when I give you the cue. (Note: T = Teacher and S = Students. Use the intonation pattern shown for each line of the dialogue.)

T: [to group A] **English is driving me crazy! driving me crazy—Repeat.**
S: driving me crazy
T: **English is driving me crazy.** [indicating with a gesture to repeat]
S: English is driving me crazy.
T: [to group B] **What's wrong?** [gesture]
S: What's wrong?
T: **Good!** [turning back to group A] **English . . .** [gesture]
S: English is driving me crazy.
T: [gesture to group B]
S: What's wrong?

T: **Repeat!**
S: What's wrong?
T: [to group A] **I thought I knew the meaning of "foxy." the meaning of foxy** [gesture to repeat]
S: the meaning of foxy
T: **I knew the meaning of foxy** [gesture]
S: I knew the meaning of foxy
T: **I thought I knew the meaning of "foxy."** [gesture to repeat]
S: I thought I knew the meaning of "foxy."
T: **Good!** [to group B] **Oh, yes. We talked about it yesterday in class. yesterday in class** [gesture to repeat]
S: yesterday in class
T: **We talked about it yesterday in class.** [gesture]
S: We talked about it yesterday in class.
T: **Oh, yes. We talked about it yesterday in class.** [gesture to repeat]
S: Oh, yes. We talked about it yesterday in class.
T: **Good!** [to group A] **English is driving me crazy.** [gesture to repeat]
S: English is driving me crazy.
T: [gesture to group B] **What's . . .**
S: What's wrong?
T: [gesture to group A]
S: I thought I knew the meaning of "foxy."
T: [gesture to group B] **Oh, yes.**
S: **Oh, yes. We talked about it yesterday in class.**
T: [to group A] **I don't understand it anymore. I got in Dutch with my girlfriend when I said our secretary was foxy. I said our secretary was foxy—Repeat.**
S: I said our secretary was foxy.
T: **when I said our secretary was foxy** [gesture to repeat]
S: when I said our secretary was foxy
T: **with my girlfriend** [gesture]
S: with my girlfriend
T: **I got in Dutch with my girlfriend** [gesture]
S: I got in Dutch with my girlfriend
T: **I got in Dutch with my girlfriend when I said our secretary was foxy.** [gesture]
S: I got in Dutch with my girlfriend when I said our secretary was foxy.
T: **Good!**
    I don't understand it anymore.—Repeat.

S: I don't understand it anymore.
T: **I don't understand it anymore. I got in Dutch with my girlfriend when I said our secretary was foxy.**
[Teacher calls on individuals, then back to gesture the group.]
S: I don't understand it anymore. I got in Dutch with my girlfriend when I said our secretary was foxy.
T: **Great!** [back to group B] **You must be kidding! She is foxy. She is foxy.**
S: she is foxy
T: **You must be kidding! She is foxy.** [gesture]
S: You must be kidding. She is foxy.
T: [back to group A] **I don't understand it anymore.** [gesture]
S: I don't understand it anymore. I got in Dutch with my girlfriend when I said our secretary was foxy.
T: [back to group B with gesture]
S: You must be kidding! She is foxy.
T: **Good!**
Yes, but which one—clever or good-looking?
[to group A] **clever or good-looking?**
S: clever or good-looking?
T: **Yes, but which one** [gesture]
S: Yes, but which one
T: **Yes, but which one—clever or good-looking?** [gesture]
S: Yes, but which one—clever or good-looking?
T: **Good!** [to group B] **Actually, both.** [gesture]
S: Actually, both.
T: **Again!**
S: Actually, both.

During the choral practice session, the students have repeated each line at least twice, and the longer lines at least three times (more if the students hesitate). From time to time the "ready individuals" may say a line before you ask the whole group to repeat it. If you hear an uneven group response, with some students doing well and others not doing well, you should allow a strong student to perform. Immediately after this student's response, ask a weaker student to repeat. Then go on to the next line; if it doesn't go well, return to the previous line or to the other group for the cue. The goal is to have each group respond to the other. A game-like challenge evolves in the process. Each time you say a line, be consistent in your pronunciation (stress and rhythm), i.e., "the music of the language." The backward build-up technique and your knowledge of stress-timed rhythm (see the "Methodology" section of this manual) will help the students learn to produce natural, native-like speech.

Finish your choral practice session by practicing the entire dialogue once or twice.

T: **Great! Now let's go through the whole dialogue without stopping. I'll start you off and cue you.**
English is . . . Come on!

S: English is driving me crazy.

Turn to the second group for its response as soon as the first group has completed the line. Continue in this way to the end of the dialogue. Try it again if you feel it is necessary.

T: **Now you know the dialogue, so let's hear from partners. Keep your books closed. I will help you if you look at me. Any volunteers?**

[When the first pair has recited the dialogue, continue with the rest of the class, expecting strong students to go before the weaker ones.]

THE DIALOGUE: PRONUNCIATION

You will need to practice the dialogue for homework. We'll have a dialogue review and test later. Practice with a native English speaker. Ask a student in the cafeteria to help you practice. It's a good way to make friends.

When you are alone, use the dialogue to work on correct pronunciation, too. In American English *basic intonation, stress,* **and** *rhythm* **are extremely important.** [Write the three terms on the chalkboard.] **First let's learn the basic intonation patterns of English. Do you know them already? Fine. Let's review them.**

Call the students' attention to the basic intonation patterns by writing the following on the chalkboard or on a transparency.

rising-falling: English is driving me crazy.
Where are you going?

downward glide: I don't anymore.
What's wrong?
I'm so sick.

rising: Are you an ostrich?
Has he gone home?

Have the students read the dialogue lines and tell you the intonation pattern for each one.

Words and syllables have stress: primary, secondary, and weak.
Here are some examples. [Write them on the board.]

primary	*primary-secondary*
Énglish	yésterdày
crázy	sécretàry
glóssary	áctuàlly

Beat out the stress-timed rhythm of the primary-secondary group.

The syllables that are neither primary nor secondary are weak; in a weak syllable, the vowel is unclear. We use this phonetic symbol to represent the weak vowel sound: /ə/, as in "but" or "son." [Write /ə/ on the board.] **Repeat this sound after me: /ə/.** [Then have the students repeat the words "but" and "son" after you.]

Choose a word from the dialogue and tell me which syllable has the primary stress. [pause for responses] **Do you see any examples of secondary stress?** [pause for responses]

Mark the primary and secondary stresses as I say each line of the dialogue. Have the students mark lightly in pencil the syllables for primary and secondary stresses. Go around the room to check their work. Next explain about rhythm (See the "Methodology" section.) Have the students mark a few spots in the dialogue that gave them difficulty during the practice session and point out the appropriate stress-timed rhythm characteristics. Assign the students' marked dialogues for home practice, ideally with a native English speaker, or with a classmate or family member. From time to time follow this procedure for marking a dialogue, but every dialogue need not be treated in such a thorough manner. Once you find the students improving in intonation, syllable stress, and stress-timed rhythm, focus on trouble spots only.

THE ROLE PLAY

Role Play

In groups of two, role-play the following situation.

Characters:
BILL   LOUISE

Situation:
Bill and Louise have been dating for a few weeks. One day Bill sees Louise having lunch with a man from her office. That evening, Bill gets very angry with Louise because he feels jealous. At first Louise thinks Bill is kidding. When she realizes how jealous he is, she tries to explain the situation.

Let's read the situation and talk about why Bill is jealous and why Louise is surprised. [Wait for the students to read the situation silently.] **Why do you think Bill is jealous?** [Elicit student responses.] **Louise thinks Bill is kidding. Why?** [Wait for student responses.]

Now let's pair up. Get a partner; the classmate sitting next to you is fine. [Try to match up a male with a female if possible.] **One of you, as Bill, will be angry and accuse the other. The other person, as Louise, will explain the business lunch and the custom of meeting over lunch with fellow workers.** [Explain this concept as needed, pointing out that the custom is especially common among white-collar workers and professionals.] **Write about five lines of dialogue. If you need help, please ask me.**

Observe the students as they write the role-play dialogues, and help any pairs who seem to need it. Give the class about twenty minutes to write the dialogue; then ask if everyone is ready. If not, give five minutes more (or a maximum of one class period). Call time and have the students read their dialogues to the class. Allow for feedback and student corrections. Make some cautious suggestions. Then tell the students they should each have a copy of the dialogue to practice at home and outside of class with their partners. At the next session they will role-play.

At the next class session, have the pairs perform their role plays in front of the whole class. Allow time for feedback about each role play.

THE DISCUSSION TOPICS

We're going to have informal discussions now. We need to get into groups. [Assist the students in moving into groups of three to five, depending on the class size. The members of each group ideally should sit in a small circle facing each other.]

OK. Introduce yourselves! Then read over the discussion topics on page 43. After you read the discussion topics, your group has to make the following decisions [write the following on the chalkboard]: **(1) which topic to discuss; (2) who will be the Group Rep; and (3) who will be the Records Keeper. Let me explain these two roles. The Group Representative will lead the discussion and will report to the class at the end of the discussion. The Records Keeper will write an outline of the main ideas from your discussion. Everyone will get a chance to be a Group Rep or a Records Keeper sometime! I will help the students who take these roles. You have ten minutes to make your decisions.**

After ten minutes visit the groups and record the names of the Group Rep and Records Keeper for each group. Also, write down the topic each group has chosen to discuss. From now on, refer to the group by the Group Rep's name.

Discussion Topics

Dealing with Jealousy: Have you ever been jealous? If so, why? What happened? How do you handle a person who becomes jealous?

Finding the Correct Meaning: Many English words have more than one meaning. When you read or hear one of these words, how can you tell which meaning is intended? When you say or write one of these words, how can you make sure other people know which meaning you intend?

Read over the discussion topic you have chosen. Help your Records Keeper write a question or statement to focus your discussion. The purpose of your discussion is to inform people about the problem; to express your agreement or disagreement with the situation; and to persuade people that the situation should either stay the same, be improved, or be changed. At the end of your group's discussion, your Group Rep will read your discussion question or statement to the class and do one of the following: give reasons and specific examples for your agreement; explain how you compromised to reach a modified statement; or tell why you decided to change the statement completely.

Your discussion question or statement should not be too general or too specific. It should sound something like this: "A jealous person should be handled in certain ways." Notice the important qualifying word "certain." Without this word, the discussion question would be too general and there would be no discussion. You would either say "yes, I agree" or "no, I don't," and you could give a hundred reasons for your opinion. With the discussion statement above, you have to discuss only certain ways to behave toward a jealous person.

Next you should define "a jealous person." Do you want to specify the sex? If so, you can rewrite the discussion question to read: "A jealous man (or woman) should be handled in certain ways." After you have discussed some ways, you may want to change "certain ways" to "three basic ways" or "two basic ways," depending on your group's decision.

Here are some examples of discussion questions based on the first discussion topic. For this first discussion, feel free to choose one of them. Next time I will expect you to write your own. [Write the following list on the board.]

1. A jealous married man should be handled in three basic ways.

2. A jealous married woman should be handled in three basic ways.

3. Jealousy between couples reveals certain psychological problems.

4. Jealousy between couples may depend on their different cultural backgrounds.
5. Louise's lunch with another man was a normal cultural phenomenon.

Remember to begin your discussion by defining the terms. Make sure everyone in your group understands the discussion question. Next, give your opinions. You have twenty minutes to discuss the issue. [Visit each group after giving them a chance to talk for five to ten minutes. Model the Group Rep's role while sitting in on a group; i.e., ask questions and use direct eye contact, to encourage all group members to participate.]

Your time is up. Let's make a large circle and listen to the Group Rep reports. There is a five-minute limit for your talks. [After each report allow time for feedback. Meet with the Records Keepers to help them write the outlines. Tell them to hand in the outlines at the next class session (for a group grade, if you wish). You may also choose to evaluate the oral reports once the students are familiar with the procedure. See Appendices A and B for speech evaluation criteria and a model outline.]

Conclude the lesson by using one of the activities from the "Lesson Notes and Activities" section of this manual.

Testing Suggestions

There are several ways to test student acquisition of content and to evaluate student progress in attaining native-like or near-native fluency. Most ESL educators choose a combination of oral production and written testing to evaluate acquisition of content, naturalness of delivery, and skill in listening. Below are some suggestions for evaluating student progress:

1. For pronunciation:
    a. Distribute typed copies of selected dialogues and have the students mark the syllables that carry primary and secondary stresses, the stress-timed rhythm characteristics, and/or intonation patterns. Each line should be read to the class only once or not at all, since the students have already practiced and memorized the dialogues.
    b. Meet with the students individually to recite a dialogue. Each private reading should be taped so that you can check later for the student's naturalness of delivery, correct intonation, stress, and rhythm.
2. For vocabulary:
    a. Distribute copies of familiar dialogues with words omitted at regular intervals. Students must fill in the blanks. See Appendix C for a model cloze test.
    b. Prepare a matching test with expressions and words in one column and their synonyms or definitions in another column. See Appendix D for a model matching test.
3. For comprehension and recall: Have the class listen to dialogues on audiocassette and respond with short answers to either written or oral comprehension questions.
4. For communicative competence: Present a role-play situation that closely parallels one practiced in class, with a list of relevant vocabulary items. Instruct the students to write a ten- or twenty-line dialogue using the information and vocabulary given.
5. For listening and comprehension: Read to the class a story rich in dialogue that contains the vocabulary and concepts you want to test. Then have the students complete a multiple-choice test or mark *true, false,* or *irrelevant* to oral or written statements.

Strictly oral testing should be supported by tape recording. Videotaping student dialogue performances is also very helpful. The tapes can immediately be played back and reviewed for both verbal and nonverbal responses. However, oral tests should only be taped if the students have become accustomed to being recorded at various times during the semester.

To be truly effective, testing should be mutual, with the students taking part in self and peer evaluation. I evaluate students on participation, timely task completion, dialogue recall, and general use of the vocabulary and expressions. In part I use tests as a psychological ploy, to make students take my course as seriously as any other. For this purpose, the speech criteria sheet—scored, graded, and returned to the student—is generally very effective.

Both in-class participation and out-of-class preparation should be part of your ongoing student evaluation. Any speech- and/or performance-oriented course requires active participation. This should be made clear at the start of the semester. Giving group grades for informal discussions should create enough peer pressure to pull the negligent loner into line. Make clear to your students at the start of the semester exactly what will be evaluated, tested, and graded.

If midterm and final examinations are required by your institution, they should include both written and spoken sections. The dialogue content, the vocabulary, the major discussion points and decisions reached, and situational resolutions created can all be tested by cloze or question-answer tests. Testing should cover the dialogue performances and role-play creation and performances. The Group Reps' reports can be evaluated, as well as the Records Keepers' outlines.

A somewhat radical means of evaluation is to have a native-English-speaking student or students come to the class for conversation and give opinions on the ESL students' fluency. This type of evaluation must be controlled by having the evaluator(s) come at the beginning of the term, at midterm, and at the end of the term.

Unit Descriptions

Unit 1: *Family Relationships*

The lessons in this unit explore sibling rivalry and sibling responsibility, relationships with in-laws, freedom and discipline for children, and respect for parents and elders. Help the students identify the underlying values and attitudes from mainstream American culture that are expressed in the dialogues. The discussions and activities encourage students to compare and contrast cultural differences in family matters.

Unit 2: *Making Friends and Getting Together*

World travelers and recent arrivals to the United States have often left behind close friends and family in other countries. In their new communities, they will meet new people and develop new friendships. The interpersonal skills and functional language used in making and keeping friends are practiced in this unit. Situations covered include thanking someone for hospitality; paying a compliment; inviting; showing concern for a friend's health and welfare; planning a party; and exchanging "small talk."

Unit 3: *Romantic Intentions*

Dating and marriage customs vary greatly from culture to culture, especially in regard to adult supervision and influence and the proper age for marriage. In this unit, students will gain insight into relationships between the sexes in the United States. They will observe the characters in the dialogues making dates, expressing interest in each other, advising friends, and paying compliments. The role plays and activities provide students with the chance to practice doing these things themselves.

Unit 4: *Being a Student*

Students in the United States must devote a lot of time and energy to studying. At the same time, school is a place that brings people together not only for study but also for socializing. Wise students learn to manage their time well and to cultivate good relationships with fellow students and with instructors. In this unit, students will explore the delicate balance of academic and social life needed to be a successful student.

Unit 5: *The World of Work*

In the United States, adults are expected to work and to care for themselves as much as possible. Work allows people to be independent; independence is a sign of adulthood and a cause for respect. Many high school and college students hold part-time jobs, working in various temporary positions until they have completed their education. High school and college graduates looking for permanent positions must know where to look and what to do. Finding a job is hard work! Applicants have to write résumés and cover letters. They must prepare to be interviewed. This unit helps students practice using job-related vocabulary and provides experience with interviewing and being interviewed.

Unit 6: *In and Around the City*

Living in a city is exciting, but it can also be confusing and tiring. This unit covers some of the realities of city life: coping with heavy traffic, getting lost, sightseeing, talking to strangers, asking for and giving directions, using public transportation, going to restaurants, and enjoying cultural events.

Unit 7: *Cultural Differences and Reactions*

The dialogues and activities in this unit present some of the similarities and differences between mainstream American culture and minority cultures in the United States. Students will have opportunities to express their opinions and to share their experiences.

Unit 8: *Recreation, Vacation, and Sports*

This unit focuses on some popular American sports and pastimes: football, baseball, camping, fishing, picnicking, and taking long car trips. Students will explain and discuss their favorite sports and pastimes.

Unit 9: *The Media*

The media includes TV, radio, newspapers, and magazines. Most people learn about local and international events through the media. In this unit, students will discuss the media and its role in their lives.

Unit 10: *Politics*

Discussing politics—whether local, national, or international—often demands some background knowledge. This unit provides opportunities for students to discuss some of the social and legal issues they are familiar with. The dialogues and activities involve comparing presidential candidates; discussing legislation to protect the environment; and debating equal rights.

Lesson Notes and Activities

UNIT 1: *FAMILY RELATIONSHIPS*
Patty, My Sister

Language Functions: describing; explaining a problem; sympathizing; showing interest; expressing disapproval

Lead-in: Ask the students if they understand and can explain the concept of "sibling rivalry." See if you can elicit any examples of sibling rivalry from the students' personal experiences. Ask the students if they and their friends talk (or complain) about how their family members behave. Why do or don't they?

Follow-up: After the students have listened to the dialogue, ask if the conversation gives them any clues to Carol's character. Do they think she might be a complainer?

Activity: (*one session*)
Tell the class that they will role-play being members of an extended family. If necessary, review the words for various relationships in an extended family (aunts, uncles, grandparents, nephews, nieces, etc.). Sketch a family tree, with names, on the board. Designate roles for the students by filling in their names on the tree.

Pass out large, blank name tags to the students. Each student should write his or her pretend name and several relationships from the family tree on the tag. The students then take turns telling about their relationships to the other family members. They should focus on how they feel they are usually treated by individual family members. The students must listen carefully to each other, since what they hear may affect what they say. The students may also enjoy role-playing a family scene involving their characters, such as a discussion about a cousin's upcoming wedding.

Baby-sitting

Language Functions: explaining a problem; expressing disapproval

Lead-in: Ask the students if their younger sisters and brothers ever misbehave. Find out what kind of behavior bothers them the most. Do they feel responsible for the way their younger sisters or brothers behave? Why or why not?

Follow-up: After the students have listened to the dialogue, ask them how they know Tom feels responsible for his kid brother. Which line gives Tom away, although he clearly feels "stuck with" his brother? (*"I won't smoke or drink. Otherwise, it's monkey see, monkey do."*)

Activity 1: (*one session*)
Ask the students how they feel about having a baby-sitter watch a younger sibling or other relative. Tell them to pretend they must hire a baby-sitter, because they have to

help an elderly relative living on the other side of town right away. However, they want the baby-sitter to follow important rules while staying in their home with their family member.

Distribute slips of paper to the students and have them make lists of "Baby-sitting Rules." Each student should cover his or her paper so that no one else sees it. The papers should be collected by two students, who will compile lists of the "do's" and "don'ts" on the chalkboard. Whenever a duplicate turns up, the student recorders must place a check mark after that rule. The check marks should be added up to find out how many students agree with each rule.

Ask the students what they think should be done with this list. Should it be placed on a wall, near the telephone, or in some other place in the house for a baby-sitter to see?

Activity 2: (*one session*)
For an alternate role play, have "Tom" display improper behavior in front of his kid brother, who imitates him, while a friend observes and advises.

The Holidays and In-Laws

Language Functions: explaining a problem; encouraging a friend; expressing impatience.

Lead-in: Ask the students to tell you their favorite holidays. Ask what they enjoy most about their favorite holidays. Explain that Christmas and Thanksgiving are the most popular holidays in the United States, even though Christmas is basically a Christian holiday. Point out that schools and public buildings are closed for these holidays, which are times for getting together with family.

Follow-up: After the students have listened to the dialogue, ask them what they think is the cause of John's problem. Is it the mother-in-law? Do mothers-in-law have a bad reputation in your students' cultures? Ask your students their opinions about mothers-in-law (and fathers-in-law). Have them give examples to support their opinions.

Activity: (*two sessions*)
Session 1: As a homework assignment, tell the students to observe a family interacting—either their own family, a friend's family, or a family from a movie or a TV show. The students should prepare to report on the interactive dynamics of the family and name the roles that people play in the family, for example: the martyr, the boss, the victim, the star, the sarcastic one, the critic, the responsible one, the irresponsible one, the beautiful one, or the strong and brave one.

Session 2: The students give their reports. Then, in small groups, have them compile lists of at least ten roles in a family. For each of the roles they must think of a representative animal or another image expressed by figurative language, such as the lion, the mouse, the whipping boy, the silly goose, the Mad Hatter, or the Cheshire cat. These lists can then be shared with the rest of the class.

Moving Out

Language Functions: expressing frustration; complaining; sympathizing; encouraging a friend; imagining the future

Lead-in: Start a general class discussion about the cultural phenomenon of generational differences—the gap that exists between parents and children. How wide is it from culture to culture? What factors affect its size? Some factors include urban vs. rural experiences; changes in political climate; and reduced or increased economic opportunities. Elicit other examples from the students.

Follow-up: After the students have listened to the dialogue, ask them if they feel their parents have a "horse and buggy attitude." Why or why not? What are some attitudes your students consider old-fashioned?

Activity: (*two sessions*)

Session 1: Have each student ask three people, each from a different ethnic background, about the two most important values they have (for example: family, show of affection, respect for age, marriage, education, success in a career or profession, honesty, gentleness, physical strength, musical talent, beauty, health). This may be done in class or assigned as homework.

Session 2: The students report on their findings individually and then compare them. For each report, they should first tell the person's ethnic background and then his or her two values. Record the information on the board for the students, and see if all the ethnic groups appear to have the same values or different ones. Discuss possible reasons for any differences. Be careful to avoid making value judgments!

UNIT 2: *MAKING FRIENDS AND GETTING TOGETHER*

A Hot Summer

Language Functions: expressing discomfort; offering a suggestion; expressing disappointment; apologizing

Lead-in: "Everybody talks about the weather, but nobody does anything about it!" Explain this expression, pointing out that many people talk about the weather, especially with people they don't know very well. Have a general class discussion about the weather, leading to a conclusion about how your students are coping with the climate of your area.

Follow-up: After the students have listened to the dialogue, ask them which season they dislike the most: the dog days of summer (hot and humid weather); a three- or four-dog night (so cold you need dogs in bed with you); windy weather; foggy weather; and so on. Ask the students what they like to do when the weather is very hot, very cold, very windy, etc.

Activity: (*one session*)

Divide the students into four groups. Set out four cards, face down. (Each card should have the name of a different season written on it.) Have a representative of each group take one card. Then tell the groups to make lists of the right kinds of clothes to wear in the season on their card. After fifteen minutes, call time and let a representative for each group tell the season and read the group's list of suitable clothing. Encourage feedback from the rest of the class. Did the group forget anything? Was something on the list that didn't fit? Have pictures available for illustration if the students ask about a vocabulary item they don't know.

The Dance

Language Functions: starting a conversation; thanking; inviting informally; boasting; paying a compliment

Lead-in: Ask the students if they have been to any parties lately. Discuss what they most enjoy doing at a party.

Follow-up: After the students have listened to the dialogue, ask them about "paying compliments." Do they think Mario and Helen are good friends because they pay each other compliments? If not, why were they flattering each other? Why do the students think Helen is worried about "hogging the floor"? Is she afraid of showing off?

Activity: (*two sessions*)

Session 1: Have the students plan an in-class dance party. Let students volunteer to bring music (tapes, records, CDs, or instruments). Make arrangements for all necessary equipment. Decide on a host and hostess who will share certain duties regarding the organization of the music—what should be played and when, and who should teach certain songs and dances.

Session 2: Have your dance party! Students who have brought music should translate the words to the songs into English if necessary, after the class has listened to the original version. The host and hostess will invite the rest of the class to join them in learning the English versions of the songs. Some "guests" should teach dances to go with the music they have brought.

Going Shopping

Language Functions: admiring; inviting informally; boasting

Lead-in: Ask the students their opinions about dressing "sharp." Elicit examples of smart or fashionable dressing.

Follow-up: After the students have listened to the dialogue, ask them if Pat likes to "put on the dog." Does Pat like having Chris show admiration? Ask the students what they think of Pat. Is she or he a sensible clothes shopper?

Activity: (*one session*)

Bring in several copies of a newspaper advertising supplement for a local grocery store or discount store. Divide the class into groups of three or four and give each group a copy of the ad. Have the students determine which buys are really good by figuring percentages and/or finding the differences between the sale prices and the regular prices on certain items. You can expand on this activity by bringing in ads from three or four different stores that include some of the same items. Give the students a list of two or three items to buy, and have them determine which store offers the best price on each item.

A Sick Friend

Language Functions: showing concern; complaining; teasing; fishing for sympathy; cheering someone up

Lead-in: How can you cheer up a friend who is sick? What could you say? Elicit examples of ways to cheer up a sick friend.

Follow-up: After the students have listened to the dialogue, ask them if they think John is dying. What is the matter with John? What are his symptoms? Then ask the students why Chris is teasing John (because John is a party animal!). Finally, ask students to explain how Chris tries to cheer John up.

Activity: (*two sessions*)

Session 1: Have the class make a list of things people can do to try to stay healthy. Let a volunteer record the list on the board. Discuss the ideas and delete any that the class votes do not belong on the list. Have the class rank the ideas on a scale of 1 to 3, assigning a 3 to the most important ways to stay healthy, a 2 to the less important ways, and a 1 to the least important (but still valid) ways.

Session 2: Before class, create and duplicate a health checklist showing the students' list of ways to stay healthy. Indicate the ranking for each item. Distribute the checklists and pair the students. The students must interview their partners about their health habits. For each thing on the list that a student does, his or her partner will award the appropriate number of points (1, 2, or 3). After the interviews, the partners should tally each other's scores and write one or two recommendations on their partner's sheet before exchanging checklists. For homework, each student could write a short essay describing his or her feelings about the activity and perhaps explaining some plans for staying healthier in the future.

Going Out

Language Functions: admiring; showing concern; describing past events; describing plans for the future

Lead-in: Ask the students if they have a friend or a relative who goes out a lot. If so, where does she or he usually go? Do your students like to dress up or "put on the dog"? Why or why not?

Follow-up: After the students have listened to the dialogue, ask them about the effects of drinking alcoholic beverages. How much is too much?

Activity: (*two sessions*)
Session 1: Plan an outing with your class. Offer practical suggestions about where to go—some suggestions might be the school cafeteria, the school grounds, or a nearby park or business—but let the class make the final decision. Then have the students write a note to you and/or the principal or director requesting permission to go on the outing. The letter should tell why the trip will be helpful to the class. When the response comes, in person or by letter, share it with the students.
Session 2: Go on the outing!

Going to a Rehearsal

Language Functions: asking for information; asking permission; giving permission; showing enthusiasm; inviting informally

Lead-in: Ask the students if they're interested in the theater and if they have seen a play recently, either at a theater or on TV. Ask them if they know any American playwrights or writers. Can they think of any plays or stories that have been adapted for film? (*In Cold Blood, Who's Afraid of Virginia Woolf?*, etc.)

Follow-up: After the students have listened to the dialogue, ask them if they know any of Tennessee Williams's other plays. If not, you might want to briefly describe the plot of *A Streetcar Named Desire* or *The Glass Menagerie*.

Activity: (*one session*)
Have the students, individually or in pairs, bring in a scene from their favorite play (in English). They should work in small groups to perform the scene. Afterwards, have a group spokesperson ask the class several questions to see if they have understood the scene and the characters. If not, a group member should explain the purpose of the scene and/or how the scene fits into the play.

An alternative approach is to provide scenes from plays yourself (some suitable choices include *The Madwoman of Chaillot, Arsenic and Old Lace, A Streetcar Named Desire*, and *The Matchmaker*). After giving a short explanation of each scene and how it fits into the play, have groups of students read the scenes. The goal of this activity is to help students to appreciate drama in English and to see it as a vehicle for learning spoken English.

UNIT 3: *ROMANTIC INTENTIONS*

A Good Time

Language Functions: expressing interest in a person; expressing disbelief; showing reluctance to get involved; exaggerating

Lead-in: Discuss appropriate ways to approach someone you want to know better for romantic reasons. Consider the effects of age on appropriate behavior. Mention some cultural differences, such as the use of a chaperone, a matchmaker or go-between, or a family member who makes the arrangements. Have the students tell about how they would like to be approached, if they had a choice.

Follow-up: After the students have listened to the dialogue, ask them what they would do if they were Henry.

Activity: (*two sessions*)
Session 1: As a homework assignment, ask the students to interview their parents or another couple about how they got together. Many married couples love to tell their romantic story. It is also interesting to note why a few don't.
Session 2: Have the students report on their interviews and compare stories.

A Hopeful Suitor

Language Functions: expressing irritation; persuading

Lead-in: Ask the students if they have heard of the English custom regarding leap year. On the 29th of February (which occurs only once every four years), a woman has the right to ask a man to marry her. Some men leave town, while others pretend they're not home when a single woman comes to the door! Ask the students their opinions of this custom. Then ask them to describe similar customs or other holidays in which male and female roles are reversed.

Follow-up: After the students have listened to the dialogue, ask them if they have ever been crazy about someone, crazy enough to make a fool of themselves. If so, what did they do? What do they think of Philip? Do they think Ann is being fair to Philip?

Activity: (*two sessions*)
Session 1: Take the class to the library, where they must work in pairs to research holidays that involve reversing the traditional male and female roles. If they have difficulty finding this information (and the librarian can't help them either), they should look up romantic customs or courtship practices instead.
Session 2: Have the partners report on their findings to the class.

The Con Artist

Language Functions: conning someone; asking for information; giving information; offering help; expressing confusion

Lead-in: Ask the students if they have ever been conned or have ever met a con artist. If so, what was that person's goal? Was any harm done? If not, elicit some examples of types of con artists to watch out for. Ask the students how they would protect a younger brother or sister against a con artist.

Follow-up: After the students have listened to the dialogue, ask them what the con artist's goal is. What does she or he mean by the statement "I have connections"? Are your students impressed by people who have friends in important positions? Why or why not?

Activity: (*one session*)
Play "Who's at the door?" One student leaves the room and stays behind the door. He or she must choose an animal and then say, "I am big" (or any other appropriate general statement). The students in the room take turns asking questions about who is at the door. Each student may ask one question and make one guess per turn; for example:
"Do you have pointy ears?"
Answer: "Yes."
"Are you a wolf?"
Answer: "No."
If the student's guess is wrong, another student takes a turn, and so on until the right answer is given. When the animal has been revealed, write its name on the board. The student who guessed the animal leaves the room and chooses another animal for the next round.

After about four animals have been written on the board, elicit expressions based on the names of these animals, referring to the glossary if necessary. Continue the game as time permits. This activity provides an excellent review of animal-based expressions.

The Engagement

Language Functions: congratulating; expressing surprise; expressing anger; accusing; apologizing; insulting

Lead-in: Ask if any of your students are engaged to be married. If not, do any of them know someone who is engaged? Ask what being engaged means. If there is no response, explain the old English and American custom of a man presenting a woman with an engagement ring if she agrees to marry him. With or without a ring, the engagement period is a time when a couple agree to be loyal and faithful to each other. At the end of the engagement period, the man and woman get married.

Follow-up: After the students have listened to the dialogue, ask which person they think has the biggest problem: Tara, Barbara, Bob, or Harriet.

Activity: (*one session*)
Have individual students or pairs of students collect information from their classmates on the details of becoming engaged in various cultures. (Who asks whom? Is there a party? Are announcements sent? Do the man and woman exchange gifts? Does the man give a ring, a pin, or something else to the woman? Does the woman give something to the man? Does the woman change her appearance in any way? Does the man change his appearance? How long is it customary to stay engaged? Who sets the date for the wedding? Is there a time limit?) As a class, compare the information collected and categorize it by cultural and familial differences.

Getting Acquainted

Language Functions: paying a compliment; flirting; expressing humility; encouraging a friend; asking permission; giving permission; leave-taking

Lead-in: Ask the students how they usually try to get acquainted with someone. How do they make friends? Would they talk to a stranger? Why or why not?

Follow-up: After the students have listened to the dialogue, ask what they think of Tom's behavior. Is Tom pushy? What kind of person is Jane?

Activity: (*two sessions*)
Session 1: Have the class work together to create a survey about what people look for in a mate. The survey should include ten to fifteen questions with multiple choice answers. Make sure each student has a copy of the completed survey. For homework, instruct the students to use the survey and interview five people about what they want in a mate. If possible, they should record whether each interviewee is male or female, married or single, and his or her age and ethnic group.

Session 2: Using the blackboard or an overhead projector, compile a tally sheet showing the responses the students received in their interviews. Discuss the results of the survey. Are any of the results surprising to the students? Analyze the results for various groups of the respondents: men, women, married people, single people, and so forth.

UNIT 4: *BEING A STUDENT*

Cutting Class

Language Functions: expressing relief; conjecturing; making an excuse; giving advice

Lead-in: Ask the students if they know what "cutting class" means. Have they ever done it? Why or why not?

Follow-up: After the students have listened to the dialogue, elicit some "good" and "poor" reasons for cutting a class. Ask the students if they think Joan is telling the truth about feeling "suddenly sick." If not, why do they think she is lying?

Activity: (*two sessions*)
Session 1: Tell the students they will have a chance to find out more about the school and its services by interviewing the principal, a teacher, or another staff member. Put on the board a list of possible interviewees and the topics each could discuss (academic and career advising, student activities, financial aid, food services, etc.) Then tell the students to choose which person they wish to interview and which subject they will discuss. Have them write out their interview questions for you to check.

Session 2: Let the students report their findings to the class.

Learning English

Language Functions: expressing frustration; expressing confusion; explaining; expressing disbelief

Lead-in: Ask the students how they feel about being a student. What is the most difficult thing about being a student? What is the most rewarding thing? Do they have trouble balancing studying with the rest of their lives?

Follow-up: After the students have listened to the dialogue, find out what they think about Mario's first statement: "English is driving me crazy!" Do they agree? Have they had any misunderstandings similar to the one between Mario and his girlfriend?

Activity 1: (*one session*)
Divide the class into groups. Tell each group to choose two people as objects of kidding or teasing; for example: mother and employer, friend and sister, or father and brother. Then have each group member list some topics for kidding or teasing each person; for example: for *mother* a student could list: *money, children, husband, house, cooking,* and *job* as topics for kidding or teasing. When the individual lists are complete, have the group choose three topics for each person and work together to think of comments based on each topic. Each group should prepare a chart of their comments that shows degrees of teasing, from very negative comments to very positive ones. When the charts are completed, have each group share its chart with the class. Encourage discussion of cultural and familial differences in kidding and teasing.

Activity 2: (*one session*)
Divide the class into groups of three to role-play the following situation. A counselor is talking to a married couple. The married couple has a problem with jealousy. Each group should decide which spouse is the jealous one and why. They ask the counselor for advice. Let the groups perform their sketches before the class. Encourage feedback from the rest of the class.

Experiential Psychology

Language Functions: expressing feelings and opinions; defending one's opinions; disagreeing

Lead-in: Ask the students if they have any knowledge of psychology. Have they taken any psychology courses? Have they read anything about psychology? What is it?

Follow-up: After the students have listened to the dialogue, ask them whether they agree with Ann or Betty. Would anyone in the class like to study psychology? Would anyone like to be a psychologist? Why or why not?

Activity: (*one session*)
Tell the students that today you are a radio interviewer. You are taking a survey of people's opinions about consulting a psychologist or psychotherapist to resolve a personal problem. Hold an imaginary or play microphone in your hand as you interview

several students. Tell the students to use phony names (famous people's names are often fun). Keep the interviews brief; for example:

> TEACHER: (as radio interviewer): Here is an intelligent-looking woman. What is your name, Miss?
>
> STUDENT: Ms. Dolly Parton.
>
> TEACHER: I am taking a survey of public opinion about going to a psychologist with a personal problem. If you felt unhappy all the time and unsuccessful in your life, would you see a psychologist to find out why?
>
> STUDENT: Absolutely not.
>
> TEACHER: Can you tell the radio audience why not?
>
> STUDENT: I don't want anyone to think I am crazy.
>
> TEACHER: Thank you. I appreciate your honesty.

Move rapidly from one person to the next. After doing about five interviews, have a student take your place. Let at least three students play the radio interviewer, and make sure every student is interviewed. After this impromptu exercise, ask the students what they learned from it. Discuss other ways of resolving personal problems (talking to friends or clergy, reading self-help books, etc.).

Problems with Studying

Language Functions: expressing frustration; sympathizing; analyzing; offering help

Lead-in: Ask the students if they have any problems with studying. Elicit some examples, and discuss some possible solutions.

Follow-up: After the students have listened to the dialogue, find out what they think Joan's real problem with studying is. What could she do to solve her problem?

Activity: (*two sessions*)
Session 1: Ask the students what an "issue" is. When you're sure they understand, present a list of issues in current politics, science, business, ecology, art, and any other fields of interest to your students. Elicit other issues from the class. Then group the students and have each group pick an issue, giving reasons for their choice and sharing with the class any information they already know about the subject. The other students may offer additional information. For homework, have the students do some library work to acquire more information about the pros and cons of their issues.
Session 2: Have the group members compile their findings. A representative of each group must then make an oral report to the class, while a "recorder" for each group should hand in a written outline of major points on the issue.

A Sick Classmate

Language Functions: sympathizing; consoling; offering help; expressing nervousness; warning; thanking; apologizing

Lead-in: Tell the students that first-year high school and college students get sick more often than other students do. Ask them why they think this is so. Discuss whether a new environment and increased responsibility and independence can lead to getting sick. Do your students believe that psychological or physical changes are most responsible for this phenomenon?

Follow-up: After the students have listened to the dialogue, ask if they have ever given a speech before a class or another large group of people. If so, how did they feel about it? What was the worst part? What was the best part? If not, would they like to have the experience? Why or why not?

Activity: (*one session*)
Divide the class into groups. Have each group act out a situation similar to the one in the dialogue. One person has a health problem, such as a headache, a sore throat, a sore arm, a stomachache, or a toothache. The other group members try to make him or her feel better by offering suggestions and consolation; for example, for a headache: "Why don't you take an aspirin? Why don't you lie down? I know just how you feel! Oh, poor you! Try not to think about it"; or for a toothache: "When is the last time you saw a dentist? I think you had better make an appointment! Maybe an ice pack will relieve the pain a bit. Let's go to the drugstore and see if the pharmacist can recommend something to help you. Believe me, I know what you're going through!"

On the Telephone: The Mistake

Language Functions: talking on the telephone; inviting indirectly; ridiculing; accusing; admitting a mistake; insulting

Lead-in: Tell the students a personal anecdote about using the telephone for the first time in a "foreign" language. If you haven't had such an experience, tell them about mine (a colleague of yours). When I lived in Turkey, I would say "allo" and then just listen as hard as I could. If I had to say something, I would just say "yes" or "no" in Turkish. (The cat got my tongue!) One solution I tried was to write out a possible telephone conversation before making a call and then read from my script. The problem was that the other person didn't always follow my script! Ask your students if they have had similar experiences with using the phone. Encourage them to share their anecdotes.

Follow-up: After the students have listened to the dialogue, ask them which person they sympathized with—Mat or Susan. Find out why.

Activity: (*one session*)
Have the students form partnerships and make lists of abbreviations and acronyms commonly used at school by students and teachers. Each pair will then put five or ten abbreviations on the board and ask the class to tell what they represent; for example:

lit = literature, OJ = orange juice, psych = psychology, P.E. = physical education, GPA = grade point average.

This activity could be expanded by having each pair or student submit a list of abbreviations for a particular subject area, such as sports (RBI), medicine (TB, mono, AIDS), or political organizations (GOP, UNICEF, NAACP).

On the Telephone: The Favor

Language Functions: talking on the telephone; asking for a favor; complimenting; persuading; showing appreciation; agreeing reluctantly

Lead-in: Ask the students if they have ever had to ask a favor of an acquaintance, someone they knew but who was not really a friend. Ask them what it felt like. Would they do it again? Why or why not?

Follow-up: After the students have listened to the dialogue, ask them what they think of Carl. Is he polite? Is he impolite or rude? How does he feel about doing a favor for Joyce? Why?

Activity 1: (*one session*)
Have the students choose products to sell to the class. They should bring some samples and pictures, and prepare to list their product's benefits or advantages to potential customers. Each student should get up in front of the class and try to persuade other students to buy the product; for example:

> Here is a wonderful toothpaste, Crest. See how carefully it is designed. You can tell how much the manufacturer cares about us. What does Crest do? Well, it cleans and protects your teeth.

After each presentation, the students should discuss what convinced them to buy and what did not.

Activity 2: (*one session*)
Have the students choose a cause to support or an injustice to protest. (They may wish to check the newspaper and TV news for ideas.) Each student should cut out newspaper or magazine articles about the topic and bring them to class, or watch the TV news and bring in information including the time, channel, and newscaster for a story to substantiate their statements. In class, each student must give a speech persuading the class to do something about the cause or injustice. Vote on which causes the class is persuaded to do something about.

The Sociology Class

Language Functions: asking for information; giving information; disagreeing; agreeing; boasting; expressing opinions

Lead-in: Ask the students if they have ever been on a field trip with a school group. If so, elicit some examples and anecdotes. If not, explain the concept of a field trip and give examples from your own experiences.

Follow-up: After the students have listened to the dialogue, find out if they have ever visited a jail or a prison. If so, elicit descriptions, initial reactions, and reflections about the experience. If not, ask if the students would be interested in such a visit. Why or why not?

Activity: (*two sessions*)
Session 1: Divide the class into teams to debate the use of capital punishment (or another topic of interest). Assign each team to read at least two newspaper or magazine articles on the topic before the next session.
Session 2: Have the debate. If the class is large, a third group can serve as the jury and choose the winning debate team. Have a prize for the winning team!

A Study Session

Language Functions: inviting informally; asking for information; arranging a meeting; giving a phone number; giving information; thanking; leave-taking

Lead-in: Ask the students if they ever study with someone or in a group. Is it a good idea to do so? Why or why not? Does it matter with whom or where they study?

Follow-up: After the students have listened to the dialogue, ask them what kind of errands Jack might have to do. What could possibly delay him and make him late for the study session?

Activity: (*one session*)
The students will give short (about one minute), impromptu talks in front of the class. Before class, prepare colored cards containing topics for the speeches. Use a different color for each subject area, such as, politics, fine arts, personal questions, travel, school, and recreation. Then write a specific topic on each card. For example, if yellow is used for recreation, each yellow card will have the name of a game, a sport, or a recreation spot. The brown cards for travel will contain the names of world cities and sights.
Tell the class which subject is represented by each color. Then let each student pick a card from the color group of his or her choice and give a short talk on that topic. At your discretion, the class may be allowed to give feedback on the talks.

The Apology

Language Functions: sympathizing; consoling; showing concern; explaining a problem; encouraging a friend

Lead-in: Ask the students if they have ever borrowed something from someone. If so, did they have any trouble returning it in exactly the condition it was in when they received it? Did any of your students ever lend something and not get it back, or have it returned in bad condition? If so, what happened? Find out how your students feel in general about lending things.

Follow-up: After the students have listened to the dialogue, ask them what they would do if they were in John's situation. Is Pat's suggestion good enough? Should John offer to pay for the book?

Activity: (*one session*)

As a homework assignment, have the students interview friends, coworkers, or other acquaintances to find out about embarrassing situations they have experienced and what happened in each case. Did they have to apologize? If so, what did they say? Your students should each prepare to report on two embarrassing situations in class. Limit the talks to three minutes, and allow time for discussion and questions.

UNIT 5: *THE WORLD OF WORK*
Looking for a Job: Before the Interview

Language Functions: giving a pep talk; agreeing; boasting

Lead-in: Ask the students if they have ever given or received a pep talk. If so, what was the situation? Talk about how athletic coaches give pep talks to their teams just before a game. Cheerleaders serve this purpose in another way.

Follow-up: After the students have listened to the dialogue, discuss the importance of self-esteem. What problems are associated with low self-esteem? Is it possible to have too much self-esteem?

Activity: (*two sessions*)

Session 1: Have the class brainstorm to create a list of topics related to a job interview (for example: proper dress, questions about previous experience and education, personal questions, impressive statements, what not to say or do, giving reasons for wanting the position, questions to ask the interviewer, getting an interview, and following up on an interview). Let each student choose a topic to research. For homework, have the students go to a school or community career development and placement office, or simply visit the library to get information about their topic.

Session 2: Each student should report to the class some tips on interviewing. For additional reinforcement you might encourage each student to do the following activity:

1. prepare and write questions for an interview in a small notebook;

2. choose a native English-speaker or a nonnative speaker who does not know your native language;

3. interview the person by asking your prepared questions and taking notes on their answers and comments;

4. report your interview to the class.

Provide students with some suggestions for beginning their interviews; for example:

"My assignment for a class is to interview someone about . . . May I ask you some questions?"

Looking for a Job: After the Interview

Language Functions: showing interest; clarifying; sympathizing; expressing good luck; offering advice

Lead-in: Ask the students if they have had an unsuccessful interview. Elicit reasons why an interview could go wrong, including mistakes the interviewee might make.

Follow-up: After the students have listened to the dialogue, ask them how they think the person ahead of Jack knew that Jack was considering another job. What effect do you think his words had on the interviewer?

Activity: *(one session)*
Divide the class into groups to role-play job interviews. Each group should decide on the kind of job that's available and the place of employment. (You could bring in want ads for them to look at to help them make a decision.) In each group, one person will be the interviewer (the personnel director or employer) and the rest of the students will be the interviewees. To show the right and wrong ways for an interviewee to impress an interviewer, at least one student in each group should model poor interviewee behavior. This can be decided by drawing lots.

Have the groups take turns conducting their interviews before the class. After each group has performed, the class should vote on which interviewee should get the job. When the votes have been tallied for all the groups, announce the results and have general feedback and class discussion.

Officemates

Language Functions: complaining; criticizing; giving examples; agreeing

Lead-in: Ask the students what kind of behavior "gets on their nerves." How do they feel about loud gum chewing, cracking knuckles, drumming fingers, coughing, sneezing, and clearing one's throat in public?

Follow-up: After the students have listened to the dialogue, ask them what was the most impolite thing George did. What do they consider really bad about his behavior, if anything? What do they think of Chris and Pat?

Activity: *(one session)*
Have the students form groups of three. Two members of each group will pretend to be having a private conversation. The third will interrupt with a story about a girlfriend or boyfriend. The original pair will try to "get rid of" the intruder. Next, have each group prepare a list of phrases or actions people might use to discourage an intruder in a private conversation.

As a class, discuss degrees of diplomacy and insult when trying to discourage an intruder. Draw this continuum on the board:

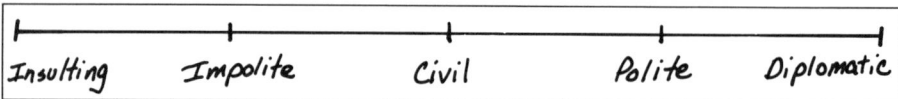

Have the students volunteer phrases and actions from their lists, and let the class decide where each one belongs on the continuum. Have a student write each phrase or action below the correct word on the continuum. Below are some examples for each category.

Insulting: (1) "Bug off!"
(2) "Get lost!"
(3) Saying anything with a sarcastic tone of voice, such as: "Would you mind not sticking your long nose into somebody else's business?"
(4) "Well, this puts a fly in our ointment."

Impolite: (1) You and your friend stop talking and move to another area.
(2) "This conversation is private, so please leave us alone."
(3) "Would you mind not intruding on our privacy?"
(4) "Excuse us, but what we are discussing is none of your business."

Civil: (1) "Hi, Tom. Well, Sara and I had better be going."
(2) You change the subject and make small talk.
(3) You excuse yourselves and leave.

Polite: (1) "Oh, Carl. How nice to see you! We were just discussing a private matter, but it can wait."
(2) "Please excuse us for a few moments. We have to discuss a personal problem, but don't go away because I have something to say to you, too."

Diplomatic: (1) "I hope you won't think I am too rude if I discuss something personal with Mattie for a bit. Please don't go too far, because I really want to talk to you."
(2) "Can you ever forgive me? Let me finish this conversation with Mattie, and then we want your advice on something."
(3) "Well, I *am* glad you interrupted our conversation. It was getting way too personal, and this is neither the time nor the place for it. How are you, anyway?"

Conclude the activity by discussing how the categories may overlap. Do the students agree on the placement of each example? Why or why not?

The Stock Market

Language Functions: asking a personal question; boasting; teasing; explaining; humoring someone; agreeing

Lead-in: Ask the students what they know about capitalism. If they can't explain it, offer a simple explanation yourself. Point out that with the stock market, anyone can buy a share/stock in a corporation. Then, when there are profits, every stockholder receives some money, called dividends.

Follow-up: After the students have listened to the dialogue, find out what kinds of businesses and/or companies they are interested in (for example: restaurants—the food preparation and service business; electronics—the manufacturing of TVs, radios, video equipment, and so on). Then ask the students if they can guess the meaning of "commodities." Generally, it refers to economics, so we might guess that Sam's father was some kind of businessman. "Commodities" may mean products of agriculture or mining. Perhaps Sam's father was selling and buying crops, farm animals, farm equipment, or mining equipment. From the title and details of the dialogue, we eventually understand that Sam's father bought and sold shares or stocks, earning money from the gains of a particular business.

Activity 1: *(two sessions)*
   Session 1: Take the class to visit the Board of Trade, a stockbroker's office, or the investment office of a local bank. Make arrangements for your field trip well in advance. The Chicago Board of Trade, for example, provides guided tours and a visitors' spot for observing the trading in action. Local banks are usually accommodating, as well.
   Session 2: Discuss what the students learned about investing and stocks during their field trip. Have the class write thank-you letters to appropriate representatives of the place you visited.

Activity 2: *(one session)*
   Use a newspaper that has an ample business/economics section to help the students understand the Dow Jones reports and other useful economic information. For instance, many students enjoy looking at the foreign exchange section to compare the exchange rates of various currencies.

UNIT 6: *IN AND AROUND THE CITY*

Traffic Jam

Language Functions: complaining; criticizing; offering advice; expressing support; thanking; agreeing

Lead-in: Find out which of your students know how to drive. Do they drive to school? Do they drive to work? Have the drivers experienced any traffic problems? Have they had any car problems?

Follow-up: After the students have listened to the dialogue, discuss the advantages of *not* driving. Do any of your students *choose* not to drive? If so, why?

Activity 1: (*one session*)
Bring in information that breaks down the cost of automobile insurance by gender, age group, type of car, age of car, and location. Present to the class and have the students draw conclusions about which groups are considered high-risk drivers. Why? Discuss laws regarding auto insurance in your state.

Activity 2: (*one session*)
Bring in road maps of your area and have the students point out the main arteries, state highways or tollways, and expressways. Discuss strategies for driving during rush hours. Review the rules of the road. Use this opportunity to point out really dangerous behavior on the road, such as how and where one can stop in an emergency. The drivers in the class can bring in their "Rules of the Road" books and share this information with the rest of the class.

Lost and Late

Language Functions: apologizing; explaining; clarifying; sympathizing; agreeing

Lead-in: Ask the students what is meant by "being late." "On time" means being in a certain place at a specified time, such as being in the room at 9:00 A.M. when class starts. Elicit other examples of places and/or events that require being on time in the United States. Then talk about events that do not require promptness, such as an open house party.

Follow-up: After the students have listened to the dialogue, ask them if they think Mat has a legitimate excuse for being late. What other excuses might be considered legitimate in certain situations? Discuss cultural differences in perceptions of timeliness.

Activity 1: (*one session*)
Pair the students and assign each pair a location that is within walking distance of the classroom and/or the school. For homework, have each pair write out directions on how to get to their location from your classroom. At classtime, have each pair orally direct another pair to their location. They should write down the directions they hear and then follow the directions in pairs. (Have a different destination for each pair of students.) When they have returned, each pair should explain to the class the directions they followed and any problems they had in finding the place. Consult the students' written directions if arguments occur over "who said what" or "who heard what."

Activity 2: (*one session*)
Choose a well-known place in town, such as a restaurant, the library, or a bank. Have each student ask one person for directions to that place from the school. Then let them report on the different kinds of directions they receive. This can lead to a discussion of how poorly or how expertly people give directions. Do age, gender, culture, or other factors affect the way a person gives directions?

The Sears Tower

Language Functions: admiring; agreeing; offering a suggestion; complaining; expressing irritation

Lead-in: Ask the students where they would go if they were tourists in your town or city. Which are the most interesting spots?

Follow-up: After the students have listened to the dialogue, ask them if they have been to the top of a skyscraper or a tower. If so, let them describe their experiences. Have they ever ridden in a hackney coach? If so, what was it like? If not, would they like to? Why or why not?

Activity 1: (*one session*)

Have the students role-play a scene in a travel agency. Two students will play a travel agent and an assistant, while the rest of the students take turns asking questions about trips to take or sight-seeing packages. Substitute the travel agent and assistant with two other students from time to time. A good way to start each conversation is for the student to state the kind of place, the length of time, and the amount of money he or she is willing to spend; for example:

"My friend and I are planning a trip to a warm climate. We have one week only, and we can spend about three hundred dollars. Can you suggest some places?"

Some useful phrases include: (1) travel by rail or train, bus, airplane, or ship (land, air, or sea); (2) one way, round trip, direct flight, stopovers; (3) tipping, gratuity included, double occupancy, vacancy.

Activity 2: (*two sessions*)

Session 1: Have the students bring in pictures from books, newspapers, and magazines of landmarks in famous cities. They could also check local travel agencies, airline offices, embassies, and/or consulates for posters and brochures. Display and discuss the pictures and the various landmarks.

Session 2: Remove the pictures. Have a student sit in the center of the class and briefly describe one of the landmarks you discussed (for example, "I'm thinking of a tall structure in Paris"). The other students must take turns asking one yes/no question apiece. After five questions have been asked and answered, the next student may guess the answer. If this person guesses wrong, the next student may either make a guess or ask another question. Continue in this way until every student has had a turn *or* until someone guesses the correct answer. The student who gives the correct answer then replaces the person in the center. If no one guesses correctly, the person in the center tells the answer and then chooses someone to be in the center for the next round.

At the Restaurant

Language Functions: ordering a meal at a restaurant; taking an order; expressing pleasure; agreeing; giving advice

Lead-in: Ask the students to recommend some restaurants for celebrating a special occasion, such as a graduation, a job promotion, an engagement, or an anniversary. Discuss the special features of each one.

Follow-up: After the students have listened to the dialogue, ask them how their families usually celebrate graduations from primary school, secondary school, and college. Is there any difference in the type of celebration and the amount of money spent for each occasion? If so, why?

Activity 1: (*one session*)
Have partners set up a restaurant with the classroom furniture. Then have each pair give a description of a particular restaurant while they walk through the mock restaurant and point out what is there: the entrance, the tables, plants, other decorations, etc. You may wish to demonstrate this with your favorite restaurant before having the students do it.

Activity 2: (*one session*)
Bring in several copies of a magazine that describes your city (for example, *Chicago Magazine*). Divide the class into groups and have each group take a section of the city, as shown in the magazine, and study the restaurants listed for that section. They should evaluate the restaurants for convenience (hours; access by public transportation), price, and type of cuisine. The group spokespersons will report to the class on what's available in their sections.

An expansion of this activity would be to vote on the most convenient, reasonable, and interesting restaurant for the class to visit. Call the restaurant to make reservations and see about a possible discount for your class. Then go and have fun!

Public Transportation

Language Functions: starting a conversation; asking for information; giving information; thanking; giving advice; expressing pleasure; expressing displeasure; admitting a mistake

Lead-in: Ask the students to describe the public transportation available in your town or city. How does it compare to the public transportation available in other places your students have visited or lived?

Follow-up: After the students have listened to the dialogue, ask if any of them have ever had to "eat crow." If so, what was the situation? How did they feel?

Activity: (*one session*)
Divide the class into groups. Each group should choose a destination in town (the house of one of the students, a restaurant, a store, a museum, the zoo, etc.) and draw a map that is large enough to display to the whole class. Have the groups take turns giving the class directions to their places, using their maps. If possible, they should also explain how to use public transportation to get to each place. The members of each group can either take turns speaking to the class or designate a group spokesperson.

The City Animal

Language Functions: expressing opinions; asking for clarification; comparing; giving examples; expressing interest

Lead-in: Tell a personal anecdote about a change in lifestyle, especially a change from living in the country to living in the city.

Follow-up: After the students have listened to the dialogue, ask them if they have experienced any similar changes in their way of living. Do they consider themselves to be city animals or country/suburban lovers? Why? Discuss the advantages and disadvantages of living in a big city, a suburb, a small town, and in the country.

Activity: (*one session*)
Bring in copies of local magazines or newspapers that describe a variety of events in the community. Have the students look for examples of plays, concerts, art exhibits, sporting events, and so forth. Then have the students categorize the events that are free to the public, those that can be enjoyed for a nominal fee, and those that are expensive. The goal of this activity is to help the students become informed about the area's offerings.

UNIT 7: CULTURAL DIFFERENCES AND REACTIONS

Introductions and Nicknames

Language Functions: introducing; asking for clarification; welcoming; clarifying; expressing pleasure; asking for information; promising; complimenting

Lead-in: Tell the students that holidays offer many opportunities to visit American families and/or participate in American events. Elicit information and examples from any students who have already had such an experience.

Follow-up: After the students have listened to the dialogue, ask them if they think Barbara is a gracious hostess. What does she say to make Tanya feel welcome? What are some other things one could say?

Activity: (*one session*)
Have one student introduce another, to the class, until everyone—including yourself!—has been introduced. Then discuss different ways to introduce people and appropriate situations for making introductions in various cultures. Does the manner of introduction depend on the status of the individual, the place, or the situation? What special means of address, both verbal and nonverbal, are used to show differences in gender and age?

Focus again on proper introductions in the United States. Ask the students how they should introduce a teacher to a family member, a friend to an employer, a classmate to a sibling, and so forth. Demonstrate and then have students demonstrate each situation, so that everyone can fully understand what is involved. Refer to the dialogue and the following examples as needed:

1. Jane: Dad, I'd like you to meet my friend, Tara Rodriguez. Tara, this is my father, Mr. Blake.
   Tara: How do you do. I'm pleased to meet you, Mr. Blake.
   Mr. Blake: I'm happy to meet you too, Tara.
2. Mary: Hi, Carl. Have you met Sylvia?
   Carl: No, I don't think so.
   Mary: Sylvia, this is my classmate Carl Smith. Carl, my friend Sylvia Stevens.
   Carl: Hi, Sylvia. Glad to meet you.
   Sylvia: Nice to meet you, too.
3. Jim: Would you care to meet my sister, Professor Tempo?
   Professor: Yes, indeed.
   Jim: Professor Tempo, this is my sister Josie. She is visiting from France.
   Professor: I'm happy to meet you, Josie. Are you going to stay long?
   Josie: I'm very happy to meet you, Professor Tempo. I will be here for two weeks.

Tell the students how important it is to repeat each person's name in formal introductions.

Being a Foreigner

Language Functions: expressing frustration; expressing culture fatigue; encouraging a friend; complimenting; expressing resignation; agreeing

Lead-in: Ask the students how they feel about being a foreigner. Did they ever feel like the foreigner in the dialogue? Did they ever get frustrated with learning English? If so, when? Why? How do they feel about the English language now?

Follow-up: After the students have listened to the dialogue, ask them if they have a friend like the American. Who cheers them up when they feel discouraged?

Activity: (*one session*)
As a homework assignment, have each student interview a friend or neighbor, if possible an immigrant or member of an ethnic minority. The students should ask three basic questions: (1) What is an American? or What does it mean to be an American? (2) What do you think is the hardest part of being a foreigner? (3) What advice would you give someone who has just immigrated to this country? Each student should report his or her findings to the class and discuss what was learned from this experience.

Women's Tears

Language Functions: criticizing; complaining; disagreeing; expressing sarcasm; explaining

Lead-in: Have a general class discussion about displaying emotions by crying, showing anger, laughing, and so forth. Do your students think it is shameful to do so in public? Do they think it's acceptable at home among family members? Why or why not?

Follow-up: After the students have listened to the dialogue, ask them to take sides. Do they agree with the man or with the woman? Is it true that "men always shrink from emotions"?

Activity: (*one session*)
Each student must describe to the class an embarrassing situation, preferably one he or she has experienced, or a fear or nightmare that is based on a bad experience. The other students must either relate a similar experience or come up with suggestions on how the experience could have been resolved or avoided.

The North and the South

Language Functions: asking for opinions; expressing opinions; comparing; describing plans for the future; expressing disapproval

Lead-in: Ask the students about regional differences in their native countries. If there are differences, what has caused them?

Follow-up: After the students have listened to the dialogue, ask them about Pat's attitude toward southerners. Do they think Pat is a northerner, a southerner, or a foreigner?

Activity: (*two sessions*)
Session 1: Take the students to the library to gather information about the customs and culture of the American South. Are there special southern dishes? Are clothing styles and music preferences different? What are some differences in the way people speak to each other? Have pairs of students gather information on various topics related to food, clothing, music, dialect, male/female roles, and other areas of interest.

Session 2: Have each pair give a three-minute talk about the topic they researched. Allow time for questions and discussion of each topic. Encourage comparisons between the American South and other cultures.

American Food

Language Functions: complaining; disagreeing; arguing; expressing opinions; inviting informally; accepting an invitation

Lead-in: Ask the students what kinds of food they consider to be "American." Do they like these foods? Why or why not?

Follow-up: After the students have listened to the dialogue, ask them to define "good food." Does it mean tasty food, nutritious food, or something else? What is the appeal of hot dogs, hamburgers, and tacos?

Activity: (*two sessions*)

Session 1: Prepare a list of American ethnic and/or regional cuisines, and assign pairs of students one type of cuisine to research in the library and/or by interviewing appropriate people. Some examples of special American cuisines include southern; Pennsylvania Dutch (German American); Cajun; Tex-Mex; soul; New England; and native American.

Session 2: Have each pair report to the class on their cuisine, using visual aids and/or demonstrating a typical dish if possible.

The Potluck

Language Functions: asking for information; giving information; describing; expressing hope

Lead-in: Ask the students if they have ever been to a feast. If so, who prepared all the food? Where was it held? What was the occasion?

Follow-up: After the students have listened to the dialogue, ask why they think Americans have potlucks. Are potlucks popular in their native countries? Why or why not?

Activity: (*two sessions*)

Session 1: Divide the class into groups. Have each group choose a table-setting custom to demonstrate; for example: American, European, rural, urban, Middle Eastern, or a special tradition of one student's family. They should prepare to demonstrate the custom to the class and arrange for group members to bring in all necessary items.

Session 2: Have each group set a table in front of the class. The group members should describe the setting, tell where it is used, and explain whether it is an everyday setting or one for a special occasion. The rest of the class should take notes. Finally, discuss the similarities and differences among the various table settings.

UNIT 8: *RECREATION, VACATION, AND SPORTS*

Staying on the Team

Language Functions: encouraging a friend; giving advice; accepting advice; expressing hope; showing concern

Lead-in: Ask the students if they have ever been on an athletic team. If so, what was the sport? Elicit some good and bad experiences your students had as team members.

Follow-up: After the students have listened to the dialogue, ask them what they think of Carol's advice to Bob. Isn't it an old-fashioned remedy? Do they think Bob will follow Carol's "medical advice"? Should he?

Activity: (*one session*)

For homework, have pairs of students collect information about a sports activity available at the school or in the community. Each pair should attempt to interview a coach or team manager for this sport. In class, let each pair report on the results of their research and interview.

Soccer vs. Baseball

Language Functions: comparing; expressing dislike; expressing confusion; disagreeing; explaining; offering help; accepting help

Lead-in: Ask the students what they know about baseball. Have they been to a baseball game? If so, where?

Follow-up: After the students have listened to the dialogue, ask them if they agree with Stella or with Joe. Do they think baseball is boring? What is their favorite sport? Do they believe, as Joe does, that Stella would enjoy baseball if she understood it?

Activity: (*one session*)

Have the students bring in pictures from magazines or newspapers (or their own sketches) to illustrate their favorite sports. Each student will explain the sport and tell why it is his or her favorite.

Camping

Language Functions: showing interest; describing past events; describing plans for the future

Lead-in: Ask the students why anyone would want to go camping. Is camping for nature lovers only? Does it appeal more to families than to singles?

Follow-up: After the students have listened to the dialogue, ask them if they have ever tossed flat stones so that they skip on the surface of the water. Describe the game of ducks and drakes, explaining that the winner is the person whose stone skips more times than anyone else's.

Activity: (*one session*)

Bring in items or pictures of items that are used in camping; for example: a tent, firewood, matches or a lighter, a lantern, a flashlight, a mess kit, insect repellent, rugged clothing, a knife, a backpack, a sleeping bag, and a first-aid kit. Have each student choose one item and explain to the class why it is useful in camping and how to use it. The rest of the class can offer help and suggestions as needed.

The Picnic

Language Functions: expressing enjoyment; making a suggestion; expressing fear; disagreeing; promising

Lead-in: Ask the students when they last had a barbecue. What did they roast?

Follow-up: After the students have listened to the dialogue, find out if anyone in the class is afraid of water. Have any of the students had or seen a frightening experience with water, swimming, boating, or the like?

Activity: (*one session*)
Have the class make a list of insects and other animals that one may encounter at a picnic. Divide the class into groups and have each group describe one animal from the list, including the damage it may cause, what to do about it at a picnic, and how to relieve its bite or sting.

Back from Vacation

Language Functions: showing interest; describing past events; sympathizing; complaining; making a suggestion; expressing pleasure

Lead-in: Ask the students when they took their last vacation. How often do they usually go on vacations? How much vacation time do they feel a person should have every year?

Follow-up: After the students have listened to the dialogue, ask them what they think about Jack's vacation. What could Jack have done to improve his trip?

Activity 1: (*one session*)
Have pairs of students read the dialogue, but change it by substituting new lines for *the Royal Palace Hotel* (where Jack stayed) and *because our car broke down* (the reason for staying). They should make appropriate changes in the rest of the dialogue, too. Then let each pair perform its dialogue for the class.

Activity 2: (*one session*)
For homework, have groups of students explore using a specific means of transportation for a vacation (plane, train, bicycle, boat, bus, and car). Each group should collect (appropriate timetables, schedules, maps, travel brochures, and travel sections from the newspaper for information. In class, each group should give a presentation about using their particular means of transportation for a vacation. They should tell about the advantages and possible disadvantages, and use visual aids to enhance their presentations.

Note: This dialogue is not well suited for choral practice due to its length. It is designed for practice with narration.

UNIT 9: *THE MEDIA*

Privacy

Language Functions: expressing opinions; agreeing; criticizing; sympathizing; expressing hope; expressing confidence

Lead-in: Ask the students when they like to be alone. Is it at any special time of day? Is it in a specific place? Are there any particular people they prefer not to be with—ever, at a certain time, or in a certain place?

Follow-up: After the students have listened to the dialogue, ask them for examples of information or situations they feel should be kept private, away from public exposure.

Activity: (*one session*)
Divide the class into groups and have each group role-play one of the following situations. Each situation involves a person being questioned by reporters. (Make up additional situations if necessary or let the groups create their own.)

1. You have just won twenty million dollars in the lottery. You don't want every relative, friend, acquaintance, and salesperson to badger you for a loan to buy something. However, the reporters want to know everything about you: your name, marital status, address, telephone number, where you intend to buy your mansion, and so forth.

2. Your house has been lost in a devastating flood, along with the houses of many others. You have lost everything, including your pets. You are in a state of shock. The reporters want to know every detail about your losses and your future plans.

3. You find out that the spouse you have been faithful to for twenty years is a bigamist. You have to go to court to testify. Your marriage has seemed normal, and you are extremely hurt and angry. The reporters gather around when you arrive at the courthouse, asking intimate questions about your marriage and how you feel about your spouse.

4. You have joined a group of people protesting discrimination at your company. You have been marching peacefully with them, but the police attack your group and drag a couple of protesters into a patrol car. Some reporters corner you for an explanation. This is a great opportunity to publicize the injustices of the company for which you have worked loyally for several years. You believe the company has paid you less than others because of your race, ethnic group, gender, religion, age, or handicap. Also, you have never been given a promotion.

The News Story

Language Functions: asking for opinions; expressing opinions; telling personal information; expressing fear

Lead-in: Ask the students if they carry a lucky charm, something to give them luck or to protect them from evil. Have volunteers show and explain their lucky pieces. If no one volunteers, show a "lucky penny," a four-leafed clover, or some other object you have brought to class.

Follow-up: After the students have listened to the dialogue, ask them about their experience with flying. How many times have they traveled by plane? How did they feel the first time? Do they enjoy flying? Why or why not?

Activity: (*one session*)
Divide the class into groups. For homework, have the members of each group watch the news on a particular TV channel. If possible, have each group watch a different channel. If not enough channels are available, some groups could report on newspapers or radio news broadcasts. In class, have each group report on the major topics or news stories covered. They should describe the organization of the news program: international, national, and local news; features; weather; sports; and any other categories. Was there a human interest story? Each group member should report on one aspect or category of the program.

UNIT 10: *POLITICS*

Democrats and Republicans

Language Functions: comparing; asking for opinions; criticizing; making an excuse; postponing a discussion; promising; agreeing

Lead-in: Bring in pictures or cartoons of an elephant and a donkey. Ask the students what each animal symbolizes. Then ask if they know of any other animals that symbolize political parties or governments; for example: the eagle (for the United States), the bulldog (for Great Britain), and the bear (for the Soviet Union). Can they guess the origin of each symbol?

Follow-up: After the students have listened to the dialogue, ask them if they can guess Tara's political leanings. Do they think she is a dove or a hawk? Why did she back out of a possible argument?

Activity 1: (*two sessions*)
Session 1: Have the class make a list of issues that would definitely affect their vote for the presidency of the United States. Write your list on the board. You may wish to include the following issues: capital punishment for major crimes; changing the minimum drinking age to 25; changing the minimum driving age to 21; prohibiting abortion; and establishing a national health-care plan. Each student should choose two issues that would affect his or her vote and write a paragraph giving reasons for the choices. Each student should read at least two articles about the issue(s) for homework.
Session 2: Have a discussion of the issues, in which the students try to persuade their classmates of the importance of their issues and the validity of their stand on each one.

Activity 2: (*one session*)
Have the students write letters to the mayor, the governor, a state representative, or other elected public official. They should express their opinions on an issue they feel is important and ask the official to take appropriate action. Provide addresses and postage if possible.

Equal Rights

Language Functions: criticizing; expressing opinions; arguing; disagreeing; expressing disgust

Lead-in: Ask the students what they know about the "battle of the sexes." Tell them that women in the United States were not permitted to vote until 1920. Women's organizations and certain outstanding individuals fought for this right for nearly a century. Today women are still working for equality in areas such as salaries and history books and school curricula. Do your students believe men and women should be treated equally? Why or why not?

Follow-up: After the students have listened to the dialogue, ask them which argument concerned them the most: women should stay home to cook for their husbands; more women should be involved in politics; fathers should help take care of their children; men should respect their mothers and wives; or women are responsible for social problems, such as youth gangs. Let the students form discussion groups to explore certain topics further.

Activity: (*two sessions*)

Session 1: Give the students a list of organizations that are concerned with equality, such as the NAACP (National Association for the Advancement of Colored People), the League of Women Voters, NOW (National Organization for Women), AARP (American Association of Retired Persons) and La Raza Unida. Have each student choose an organization and research its history, goals, and accomplishments during a class trip to the library.

Session 2: Have each student report on the name of the organization, how old it is, how many members it has, and its goals and accomplishments. After the reports, have each student tell which of the organizations he or she would like to join and why.

Appendix A
Criteria for Evaluating Oral Reports

The following checklist can be used for your evaluation of students' oral reports. Before beginning the speeches, distribute copies of the checklist and explain it to the students. It is recommended that you assign each category a maximum of twenty points, for a possible total score of one hundred. After the speeches, meet with the students individually to discuss their evaluations.

I. Introduction

+ commands attention of group (attention-grabbing statement, waiting and using eye contact, initial and effective use of visual aid)

+ shows motivation and clear purpose

− apologizes

− insults or offends   score: _____

II. Appearance

+ is dressed and groomed appropriately for the situation

+ uses appropriate gestures, movements, and posture

+ uses visual and/or audio aids creatively and logically

− makes distracting movements   score: _____

III. Audience Contact

+ meets several people's eyes at varying times (has good eye contact)

+ uses note cards effectively or has no need of them at all

+ refers to the audience members and/or includes them in the presentation

+ shows poise, naturalness, and keen audience awareness

− is paper-tied   score: _____

IV. Vocal Factors

+ uses correct time-stressed rhythm and intonation with a minimum of mispronounced words

+ uses appropriate pitch, rate, loudness, and variety of voice with good pacing and timing

− speaks in a monotone

− speaks too fast

− speaks inaudibly or unclearly; cannot be comprehended

− makes distracting sounds score: _____

V. Subject Matter

+ creates audience interest in the subject or uses a well-chosen subject that interests the audience

+ shows preparation and thinking; i.e., has obviously "done the homework"

+ shows organization and sense

+ uses correct grammar and appropriate vocabulary for the most part

− gives irrelevant information

− is confusing score: _____

Total: _____

If the speech or talk was intended to persuade, was it effective? _____

(Did the majority of the audience respond "yes" to this question?)

_____

General Comments and Suggestions:

_____

_____

_____

Appendix B
Records Keeper's Model Outline

(This model outline is for the discussion topic, School Rules and Regulations, in Unit 4, "Cutting Class.")

Group Members' Names: Ricardo Montalban, Richard Dreyfus, Greta Garbo, Mata Hari

Discussion Question: What kinds of rules and regulations should our school have?

I. Dress Codes
   A. Propriety
   B. Sloppiness
II. Health Hazards
   A. Smoking
   B. Drinking alcohol
   C. Littering
   D. Roller-skating
III. Disturbances
   A. Radio playing
   B. Shouting and whistling
   C. Roughhousing (horsing around)
   D. Lovemaking
      1. kissing
      2. holding hands

Group Decisions: This outline shows the kinds of student behaviors that should be regulated by the college. The group unanimously supports strict rules against smoking, drinking alcoholic beverages, littering, and roller-skating. In addition, activities that cause disturbances such as radio playing, shouting, whistling, horsing around, and displays of lovemaking should not be allowed on school grounds. However, group members disagreed about the dress codes. Two members believe that in the hot summer months wearing shorts and t-shirts is okay. The other two members believe that the wearing of shorts should be banned. We all agreed that students should be required to wear shoes, since bare feet can spread dirt and disease. We decided that a committee of professors and students should be formed to write out specific rules based on the major topics in our outline.

Appendix C
Model Cloze and Vocabulary Matching Tests

Cloze

(Note: This model cloze test is an example of a teacher's discretionary use of the general rule of omitting words at regular intervals. When putting together cloze tests, you will need to consider the students' capabilities and the lessons covered in class. Generally, when omitting words, you should consider both content and function words and sentence structures.)

Directions: Fill in the blanks with words that fit logically and grammatically.

A. Family Relationships: Patty, My Sister

    Carol's sister Patty is very _____. She is sixteen years old, _____ she still wears _____ and chews her fingernails. _____ not only lives high _____ the hog, but also she _____ not have a part-time _____. When her mother told _____ to get work, she just _____ more money out of her mother. Carol believes her sister will also _____ out of looking for a job.

Answers: childish, but, pigtails, She, off, does, job, her, wormed, weasel

B. Romantic Intentions: A Good Time

    Henry thought Sam looked like a _____ in a hen house at the _____. Sam had so many _____. However, the one he _____ to see again wasn't interested _____ him. Sam tried to _____ out some information about her. _____ sounded like a lot of _____ to Henry. Henry was even _____ surprised when he found _____ Sam liked his sister the _____. Sam thought it was too _____ to be true and asked Henry to _____ a meeting. Henry said that his _____ was usually on her high _____ and that he had never tried to _____ her up with anyone. _____ planned to tell her what a _____ Sam was. It seems that _____ now on Sam may _____ on Henry's sister.

Answers: fox, party, girlfriends, wanted, in, ferret, That, bull, more, out, best, good, arrange, sister, horse, fix, Henry, peacock, from, call

A cloze test may be simplified by giving the students choices for each blank; for example (for paragraph B above):

1. a. dog   b. fox   c. cow
2. a. party   b. drugstore   c. office
3. a. relatives   b. problems   c. girlfriends
4. a. hated   b. wanted   c. let

Vocabulary Matching

Directions: Match the words and expressions in column A with the definitions and synonyms in column B. Write the letter of the correct definition after each number.

Example: albatross __e__

A

1. get on my nerves _____
2. clam up _____
3. line up _____
4. sheepish _____
5. dog-eat-dog _____
6. bearish _____
7. piggy bank _____
8. wolf down _____
9. pull out _____
10. bullish _____

B

a. plan or arrange
b. rough and gruff
c. positive; good
d. brave
e. a weight; burden
f. wait a minute
g. quit
h. irritate or bother
i. wet and sticky
j. get quiet or speechless
k. a container for saving money
l. having hard and cruel competition
m. gobble up; eat fast
n. passive; shy